In memory of Mike McHugh,
who always thought of the children first.
He listened to parents, valued his staff,
and insisted we work together
to improve the lives of our students.
He exemplified all that was right
in the field of special education.

And to our women friends
who provide a shoulder to lean on
when times are tough.
They are the first we call when
something wonderful occurs
or when we are in the pits of despair
and can't see the light.
Together we can be vulnerable,
unreasonable, silly, mad as hell,
or full of joy.

Susan Magers and Donna Spencer have written a "pot of gold at the end of the rainbow" book for parents of children requiring special education. Clear, compassionate, practical, and based on real experience, it offers what, in my view, virtually every parent needs to understand. In 1968, we, at the new Federal Bureau of Education for the Handicapped, asked the White House and Congress for an authority to provide information to parents of children with disabilities. We used the funds to organize data on where special education programs were available at the time. Our early experiences demonstrated that parents needed more than directions to programs and fact sheets, and so we began making grants to parent groups to be models for individualized help. Magers and Spencer are the evolution of that effort, and their book is "the pot of gold..."

Edwin W. Martin, *First Assistant Secretary of Education for Special Education and Rehabilitative Services U.S. Department of Education, 1979-81*

Sound advice. Life changing. Buy it. Read it. Live it.

Sue Memminger, *Mom*

Susan and Donna's expertise in advocacy has helped get our children where they needed to go to become happy, independent, and successful students. We went from feeling frustrated, isolated, and deflated to empowered, understood, and confident with the wisdom contained in this book. When you are ready to move your mountain, consider this book your sherpa of advocacy assistance!

Kathy James, *B.A., B.S., R.Ph., Mom*

Learning how to work collaboratively with a school to access appropriate services for your child can be extremely challenging. *Moms Move Mountains* is the perfect how-to book to help advocate for your child's unique needs. The authors share authentic experiences which will be a gift to any parent or caregiver who can use the wisdom gained through firsthand knowledge.

Kim Kiernan, *M.S. CCC-SLP*

Moms Move Mountains is a book every parent of a child who learns differently needs to have! Finding the right menu of educational and emotional supports for your child can be a confusing, daunting, and never-ending process. The authors have used their extraordinary background as educational advocates to provide much needed guidance in an understandable format. Their content choices are carefully crafted to allow you as parents to truly become an active and collaborative voice in your child's education. As an expert in autism spectrum disorders for over 25 years, I know that this book will become a resource that I share with parents over and over again.

Sylvia F. Diehl, *Ph.D., CCC-SLP*
University of South Florida
Communication Sciences and Disorders Department

As a classroom teacher for thirteen years, I knew the challenges I would face as a mother of a child with special learning needs. Susan gave me the tools I needed to turn my fears into productive steps and successful results. As my son grows and changes, so will his needs, but I feel better equipped to advocate for the support he will need to be successful in the classroom. Today, my son is happy and thriving. I can't recommend Susan's methods more highly.

Andrea Tirabassi, *Mom*

Susan Magers is a pioneer in advocating for ESE students and parents. She is extremely knowledgeable, compassionate, and forthright in dealing with school officials during IEP meetings, care meetings, etc. Susan is the woman we, parents, go to when seeking answers to IEP questions and when we need help navigating the school system. Susan is the woman I hope to emulate during my child's school years. She is my hero!

Debbie Ezelle
PTSO President Oak Park School
for students with special needs
in Sarasota, FL

I first met Susan Magers when my daughter, Trinity, who has Down syndrome, was still in preschool. Susan was our first contact with a parent advocate. She was an inspirational, compassionate, resourceful leader who provided exceptional service toward awakening Trinity's potential and making them into reality. Trinity is now 16 soon to be 17 and is becoming those dreams and she affirmed for the first time Saturday, "I am an adult."

Linda Lilly Kranz, *Mom*

Working with students at risk of not earning a high school diploma, I have seen the tremendous impact knowledge of the special education system has for parents. It leads to best outcomes for the students. The tools presented in this book are like having a special education professional sitting next to you as you interface with school staff on behalf of your child.

Jaye Williams
Director of Religious Education

One of our daughters was diagnosed with a serious visual disorder. If she was to remain in the regular school system, changes needed to happen within the classroom. As we encountered road blocks we realized that we needed a better understanding on how to advocate for our child. Susan Magers played a key role in educating us on how to acquire this knowledge, which has allowed us help our daughter be successful.

Teresa Bencie, *Mom*

Susan and Donna are a knowledgeable asset for any parent who needs help navigating the complex and ever-changing area of special needs education. This book should be on reading lists for all disability education organizations and advocacy groups.

Deb Hobson, *Mom*

Published by Bardolf & Company

MOMS MOVE MOUNTAINS
Special Education Survival Skills for Parents

ISBN 978-1-938842-30-6

Copyright © 2016 Susan Magers and Donna Spencer

For information write:

Bardolf & Company
5430 Colewood Pl.
Sarasota, FL 34232
941-232-0113

Printed in the United States of America

Cover design by Shawcreative

MOMS
MOVE
MOUNTAINS

Special Education
Survival Skills
for Parents

Susan Magers and **Donna Spencer**

Bardolf & Company
Sarasota, Florida

Contents

... She can feel it down to her core—
this is her time. She will not only climb
mountains—she will move them too.

—Lang Leav

Preface

Our story began in 1975. Two monumental events took place that year. On November 30, 1975, Gerald Ford signed PL 94-142, the Education of All Handicapped Children Act into law. This was the first time students with disabilities were guaranteed equal access to education.

The other big incident that happened was Donna's son getting kicked out of the kindergarten class at his private school in Sarasota, Florida. Donna had just passed her exam to be a realtor when she received a call to come to school for a meeting. When she got there, the principal bluntly told her that her son's behavior was out of control, he had a learning disability, and he could not remain in their school.

Donna was understandably upset, angry, and confused. She and her husband paid tuition through the end of the quarter, and she felt her son had a right to continue to go to the school. The next day she took him back and tried to drop him off, but the school refused to keep him and told Donna to take him to his assigned public school.

Special education services in the public schools were just beginning to be offered, and many people in the community did not think they were adequate. Even the head of the Special Education Department, who was Donna's friend, told her to look for other education options. But there weren't any, so Donna reluctantly enrolled her son in public school.

She quickly realized she was going to have to take an active role in her son's education so he would get the services he needed to succeed. She started advocating for him at his local school and became involved in a parent group at the district level so she would have a voice in policy decisions. Donna was fortunate to meet other like-minded parents who helped support each other.

In 1989, the parent group wrote a grant and started the Parent Liaison Program. Donna successfully applied to become one of the two parent liaisons. Their mission was to help other families of children with disabilities understand the special education process and to attend Individual Education Plan (IEP) meetings with them. There was minimal training provided, essentially the two parent liaisons were told, "You know what to do—go do it." This parent-to-parent education program ran successfully for more than 20 years.

Susan's journey started in 1997 when she and her husband took their oldest son to orientation for kindergarten. His little sister tagged along. As they made their way through the various registration stations, a staff member introduced them to the speech-language pathologist, who asked if either child had been evaluated for language concerns. Susan and her husband were surprised parents and replied that they hadn't. Within the year, both children were diagnosed with disabilities, Susan's son with language impairment and attention deficit hyperactivity disorder, and her daughter with autism.

While living in Maryland, Susan recognized that it was important to get involved at her children's school. The IEP process felt overwhelming at first, but she found that it worked better when she forged relationships with her school partners. Susan joined the PTA and eventually became the volunteer coordinator for the school.

However, life as their family knew it had changed forever. Over the course of the next few years, Susan left her well-paying job, she and her husband opened their own business, expenses skyrocketed, and their only option was to file for bankruptcy. The family decided to move to Florida for a fresh start. After their arrival, Susan immediately started looking for opportunities to be part of the school community.

She became the room mother for her son's class, joined the PTO, and became involved with the Legislative Committee at the district level. She also attended a parent training course on autism offered by the local university. It turned out that Susan was the only parent who showed up for the training, so instead of being part of a conventional class she was able to sit and chat personally with the trainers. They told her about a new program that employed parents as local community-partners. Susan applied for the job and started working with other families that had children with autism.

In late 2001, the Parent Liaison Program was looking to hire two new parents, and one of the school district employees recommended Susan. She applied and was hired. That's how she met Donna and began their long-standing partnership.

Over the last 15 years, Donna and Susan have become the best of friends, traveled the country together, and helped thousands of families advocate for their children. In 2008, they left the Parent Liaison Program and started their own private advocacy firm, *Pave the Way Consulting*. Although they closed the business after a few years, they continued to offer parent workshops.

In order to capture our collective knowledge gathered in many years of attending IEP meetings with families, we decided to write this book. We are proud to present to you, *Moms Move Mountains: Special Education Survival Skills for Parents* with the hope that it will inspire, educate and empower you to navigate the public school system for your own child.

Susan Magers & Donna Spencer
Sarasota, Florida 2016

A note on the title of the book: Although we are well aware that many dads participate actively in their children's education these days, in our experience, nine out of ten of the people we encounter and help in our work are moms. We encourage fathers to get involved whenever possible, and trust that *Moms Move Mountains* will be helpful for them, too.

Introduction

Parents have become so convinced that educators know what is best for children that they forget that they are the experts.

—Marian Wright Edelman, educator

When you have a child with disabilities in public school, you'll be asked to go to many Individualized Education Program (IEP) meetings, and you're likely to become a veteran, as we did. But attending your very first meeting can be one of the scariest things you'll ever experience as a mom. You are summoned to the school to meet with a large group of people who want to discuss your child's difficulties.

Then you are handed a long, legal document with tiny print outlining your parental rights. It would be nearly impossible to read and comprehend in the comfort of your own home, but trying to do so while everyone stares at you, impatient to begin the meeting, is quite daunting.

Next, you are introduced to people with strange sounding titles like Occupational Therapist and Speech-Language Pathologist. Most of the people look friendly enough, you may have even met them once during the evaluation phase, but it still feels a bit overwhelming as you try to process all the new faces and figure

15

out what they do and why they are in this meeting. Some of them like to use educational jargon, unfamiliar words, and bewildering acronyms and abbreviations.

The person leading the meeting starts reading off information about your child. This is more familiar territory—student's name, address, and birthday. Yep, you know all of those.

The next question that may be asked is, "What's your child's exceptionality?" You get that they're looking for the label that tells everyone how your child is different. Not quite sure how you feel about labels but realizing they apparently are necessary to get your child services, you mumble some sort of answer.

Then the team leader looks at you as says, "What are your concerns for your child that you want addressed during the next IEP year?"

In your head you are thinking, "Nobody told me I was expected to have answers. I thought they were the professionals. I was supposed to have a list of concerns?"

But they are all sitting there looking at you. So you start to think about ways in which your child struggles. You come up with a reply: "Johnny seems to be having a hard time paying attention in class and he has difficulties making friends with his classmates. Maybe we all could help him with those challenges?"

Everyone nods and the team leader fills in the parent's concerns on the IEP document. That leads to a review of Johnny's present levels of performance, which tells everyone how he is doing in class right now and summarizes the results of all the testing that was done to find him eligible for special education.

A "draft copy" of the IEP document that shows the goals the school team is recommending is handed out to everyone. It's the first time you have seen it. The special education teacher has written a goal to work on reading strategies; the speech-language pathologist (SLP) has written a goal to work on the W questions— What, When, Who and Why; and the occupational therapist (OT) wants to start a handwriting program so that Johnny can write more legibly. After all the goals are read you're asked you if you agree. You think, "Well, they are the professionals and if they think this is what we need to do, who am I to disagree?" and say, "yes." Great!

Moving right along, Johnny will receive assistance in reading by going to the special education teacher two times per week for 30 minutes; he will see the SLP two times per week for a total of 45 minutes; and the OT will see him two times per week for 15 minutes. This is followed by a short list of accommodations, which includes repeating directions, reading questions out loud, and allowing extra time to complete assignments and testing. If Johnny has to take any type of standardized testing, his teachers will not be able to read the questions to him because that is against the rules. If you agree, please sign here.

Could you also sign here that you were present in the meeting; here where it states that you were not discouraged from bringing someone with you; here where it says that we gave you your procedural safeguards; and here that you agreed it was OK with you that the principal was invited to the meeting but was unable to attend? So you sign, sign, initial, sign and sign some more.

When you are finished, the team leader says, "Thanks so much for coming today. We will make a copy of the IEP and send it home in Johnny's backpack. Please call us if you have any concerns, and, if not, we will see you next year."

You walk out the door with your head spinning. What just happened? You expected this would be a long meeting where the team would explain everything to you in detail. Then you would work together to decide how to best help Johnny. As you look at your watch, you realize only 20 minutes have elapsed and you aren't even sure why you were invited to the meeting. It seemed like the team had already decided what to work on and they really only needed you there to sign various pages of the form.

Have you had a similar IEP meeting experience? Did you feel like a true part of the team or that you were only invited because the law requires the school to give you notice of the meeting? Were your concerns for your child addressed in the IEP or had the team pre-determined the priority needs?

If you have had this experience or similar encounters and you want to know how to feel more in charge of your child's education, this book is for you.

Over our twenty-year experience dealing with school systems and supporting parents of children with disabilities, we have learned a great deal and want to pass our knowledge on to you. Just as we learned from those who went before us so we didn't have to start from scratch, you can build on the wisdom we have accumulated.

What it boils down to is that you need to become an advocate for your child. You must seek the knowledge to help him or her to be successful. You need to do the best you can do each day and try not to beat yourselves up for what remains undone. You must have a plan to guide you while still taking time out to enjoy the journey.

This may require you to change your mindset considerably. It is essential for you to be in control of your emotions and think logically while you are working your way through the many complex situations that arise as you raise a child with a disability. You need to think about the future and how the decisions you make today may influence the opportunities your child will have tomorrow.

You need to learn how to manage the many pieces of information that will come into your home as you work with doctors, therapists, and educators to help your child. Inevitably, problems will arise and you will need a process for resolving the issues.

One of the greatest resources for children and families is the school. You will learn that it takes time and persistence to work with the school system successfully. You need to get to know the players, policies, and politics. You will need to set aside time to prepare for and attend meetings on your child's behalf.

You will also obtain a thorough understanding of the IEP process and your role in working with the schools to appropriately educate your child.

How to Use this book

We recommend that you read it all the way through, including the appendixes. This will give you a good overview. Then go back to the chapters that deal directly with your immediate concerns.

Every profession and government agency has its own lingo, and the special education field is no exception. If you come across any unfamiliar terms, please refer to the extensive glossary we have provided in Appendix B.

At the end of each chapter is a "Highlights" section, which bullets the main points covered.

This is followed by a "Getting Ready" section that has various projects related to the issues addressed in the chapter. We urge you take the time to do them. Going through the process will prepare you so that you can advocate for your child with optimal chances for success.

Chapter 1

Dealing with Emotional Stuff

The beginning of a journey is a terrible time to plan. it's the moment of greatest ignorance. In self-directed education, a lot of the value comes from exploiting opportunities that arise well out to sea, once I've seen some things and begun the learning process.

—James Marcus Bach, author and consultant

Before we get into how to work with the school district and write an IEP, we want to take a step back and talk about emotions. For many families, finding out a child has a disability or learning difference can be scary, frustrating, and overwhelming. Mothers and children are connected. When your child struggles, you feel it in your soul. It churns up your feelings, it can affect your other relationships, and it may even trigger the grief cycle. In other words, you may feel like a mess. To start the clean-up process you must take care of yourself, learn about the effects of grief on you and your family, and start to build a support network.

Taking Care of Yourself

Many parents work tirelessly on behalf of their children with disabilities, but it can take a heavy toll. Studies show that mothers of children with significant disabilities have the same level of stress hormones as combat soldiers. They also have poorer physical health and more incidents of depression which can lead to negative long-term effects on memory and cognitive decline.

Caregivers often experience guilt when taking time for themselves, but it is important to look after your own needs, too. Give yourself permission to take care of you! Rest, relaxation, and heck—even a dose of heel kicking fun, will give you the emotional and physical energy needed to take care of your child with a disability and the rest of your family.

Here are a few ideas of things you can do to take care of yourself:

Make Connections: Moms of children with disabilities often feel very much alone, as if they are the only ones having this experience. However, if you look around, you'll soon figure out this is not the case. You'll find other moms who have experienced similar emotions. After making those connections, you'll start to calm down. Feelings of isolation will diminish.

Find Solutions: Concentrate on solving problems. Seek solutions by asking questions, doing research and putting your situation in perspective. This process takes time, but it eliminates stress as you start to regain a measure of control.

Seek Assistance: You can't do it all. Seek assistance with daily activities and accept help when it is offered. You don't have to be Superwoman.

Maintain Health: Take care of your physical health and wellbeing. Make sure to get as much rest as possible. Don't use eating as way to cope. Too much food, or not eating at all, can sap much needed energy. Getting regular exercise will help you stay fit and feel better mentally.

Avoid Blame: Don't place blame on yourself or your husband for having a child with a disability. Constantly trying to figure out what caused it drains you. A lot of time and money can be wasted trying to answer "Why me?" and "Why my child?"

OK. So, you are following all of this advice, taking time out to care for you: eating well, exercising regularly and staying connected.

Then why do you still feel so terrible?

The answer is likely to be: Grief. Finding out that your child has a disability can plunge you headlong into the grieving process. We all have hopes and dreams for our child's future, but now your dreams are shattered. You are grieving not only the changes in your child's future, but your own. You may start out in denial; then feel angry, shocked, fearful, guilty, depressed, or anxious. There are suddenly many unknowns. You may feel out of control. The more significant the loss, the more intense the feelings seem to be. Special events, like birthdays and anniversaries, can trigger a recurrence.

Managing Grief

How do you pick up the pieces? The grieving process has no set timeframe. You can't hurry it along, but you can prolong it by not accepting it. Let the grieving process unfold naturally. Friends and family may not always know how to react, but holding in feelings can have a negative impact both physically and emotionally. Share your feelings with someone who can help you sort through the emotions and find coping strategies.

The most important factors to help you heal from a loss are getting enough rest, eating right and seeking support. Accepting offers of help with day to day activities from others helps, too.

Eventually, you will start to cope and have hope again. The darkness of grief will begin to lift. Glimmers of light and laughter will slip back into your life.

Above all, you will have that first moment of joy that only a mom of a child with disability can experience. If you have been doing this for a while, you know what we're talking about… Your five-year-old makes eye contact with you for the first time, ever. Your seventeen-year-old learns to tie her shoes. Your middle schooler who seems to ignore the world gently places a bandage on your scraped knee. Your fifth grader reads a whole sentence - without assistance.

What about the child with hidden disabilities—the ones you can't see like AD/HD and learning disabilities. You start doing the happy dance when your child turns his homework in on time, in the right basket, without a reminder.

If you only have typical children, those small accomplishments may be no big deal. The little things do not have monumental importance. But we know the small things matter. Every time our child has a successful moment, we celebrate. What other parent would do the happy dance for getting homework in on time?

By the way, dads experience grief too. So, your husband may feel similar emotions but experience them at different times than you do. We all experience grief in our own unique way. It is difficult to support each other if you are both going through the grieving process. Be kind to each other. Cut each other some slack.

Family Relationships and Friends

Has your relationship with your husband changed? Do you agree on how to help your child with a disability or have you pushed each other away as you try to deal with your separate emotions? Men and women often react differently to trying situations and have different approaches in working through a new challenge. Statistics show that 80% of couples who have children with disabilities end up divorced. We urge you to carve out quality time with your spouse. Go to dinner. See a movie. Have sex! Yes, we know your life will never be the same, but getting back into a "normal" routine can help you learn how to live again.

Siblings of children with disabilities often report feeling angry or left out because they no longer have enough of their parents' attention. Look for opportunities to have one-on-one time with your other children. Explain to them, in terms they can understand, about their brother's or sister's disability. Find family-centered solutions to the new challenges in your home.

Here are a few examples of family-centered solutions. We're sure you can come up with many more if you consider how needed changes will impact your entire family, not only the child with a disability.

If one of your children struggles with following verbal directions, instead of creating a chore list just for that child, make a family chore chart and the written reminders will help everyone. Maybe you have a child that struggles with loud noise or bright lights and they need a low input space. Have everyone in the family decide where the quiet space should be in the house and help with the decorating decisions to make the room sensory friendly. Make this a family space rather than isolating the child with special needs.

Many school guidance counselors offer a support group for siblings of children with disabilities. Some disability organizations have "sib shops" specifically designed to help siblings without disabilities understand their emotions related to having a brother or sister with a disability.

The relationship with your extended family may also change once you have a child with a disability. Grandparents, aunts, uncles and cousins may not know how to react to the news and will need your help to understand. The same goes for friends.

Some people are uncomfortable or afraid and may cut off contact with you. Others offer unsolicited advice and may overwhelm you in their efforts to be supportive. In the best case scenario, your extended family members and friends will understand that you are going through a period of adjustment and will follow your lead.

Make an effort to educate your family and friends with the facts about the disability, how it impacts your child, and what help you have decided is required. Let them know what they can do to be of assistance. But realize that some may experience grief over the situation themselves and be unable to support your needs.

Try to maintain good relationships with your extended family and friends, but in the end, they must own their emotions and responses. If someone causes you more harm than good, then maybe you need to distance yourself from that person, at least for a while, if not for good.

Building a Support Network

One piece of advice we give to everyone we work with is to build a support network. You cannot do this alone! You need to talk to people who listen with empathy. Surround yourself with others who have walked in your shoes because they can provide assistance, information and ideas.

Where do you find this support network? Many people start with family members and close friends; people they trust. But it may also include a teacher, therapist, member of the clergy or medical professional. It looks different for each person.

So make time to have coffee with your sister, or call your best friend on the telephone. Keep the lines of communication open and remain engaged in your social relationships. Do not become isolated while you figure out your new life; continue to reach out.

Maybe you live in a new community far from your family. Look for friendships at work, at your place of worship, or at your child's school. If you have a talent or interest, find a group that meets to pursue those interests and try to connect with its members. Surrounding yourself with other people helps to combat stress, boosts your wellbeing, increases your sense of self-worth and provides comfort. Having a support network means you are not alone.

There are also support groups specifically for parents of children with disabilities. These types of groups allow you to connect with other moms who may be experiencing similar issues. Participating can give you the inside scoop on available community services, schools that do a good job with students with disabilities, and links to other disability-related resources. Some parents attend a support group meeting only once or twice, others meet lifelong friends and participate for many years. Give it a try and see if it works for you.

Disability Professionals

Along with a disability diagnosis, a host of new professionals may enter your family's life. It could be a social worker, speech therapist, mental health counselor, or special education teacher. These are people who are paid to help your child and often become part of your support network. You may build lasting relationships with some of them in the process. They start out as professionals but wind up as friends.

Family, friends, co-workers, community members and paid professionals form the multiple layers in your circle of support. Keep your family connected to the community by accepting assistance and avoid feeling like you must do everything on your own.

Cindy's Story

Recently, a mom named Cindy called us for help to find an appropriate school placement for her son Charlie. Charlie was seven years old and had multiple physical disabilities and a seizure disorder. The family had just moved to our community and Cindy was worried that the school district could not meet Charlie's needs.

Realizing that she needed information from local experts in order to make a good decision on school placement, she called one of the disability service providers in town that referred her to us to discuss her options. It was the first time Cindy had ever talked to another mom of a child with a disability, and we spent a long time on the phone together. By the end of the conversation we could feel Cindy's stress level diminish. She expressed a sense of relief to know that she was not the only person to have such worries for her child and that her emotions were quite normal for a mom of a child with a disability.

We talked about her support network. Cindy had no siblings, her parents lived in Europe, and her husband had a job that required the family relocate to a new city every two years or so. Charlie's medical issues were significant and he needed care twenty-four hours a day. Cindy had spent the first several years of Charlie's life in and out of hospitals and interacting with many different medical specialists. As he got older, she and her husband hired a live-in nurse to help provide care for Charlie.

Cindy was very open to meeting new people and building a support system in her new community. We gave her information on a local support group for parents of children with cerebral palsy. At the school Charlie would attend, we introduced her to the president of the PTA, who also happened to have a child with a seizure disorder. Finally, we connected her to a church in her area that welcomed families of children with disabilities and provided accommodations for the children to be included in activities. It took some work for Cindy to establish and nurture these relationships, but she understood the value and invested the time it took to make these connections.

Interacting with the School System

Unfortunately, the world does not stop when you are dealing with your initial emotions and reactions to having a child with disabilities. In some cases, you must interact with the school system while coping with your grief. Feeling anxious, fearful, angry and guilty can make it difficult to function. When you are in an emotional state, you may not communicate effectively. Avoid alienating those who are trying to help you and quickly apologize if you feel like you may have offended someone.

Sometimes you need to set aside your emotions in order to be an effective advocate for your child. You know that anger and blame will not serve you well when you are seeking services for your child. Give yourself and everyone else a break.

Recognizing and dealing with your emotions allows you to be more helpful to your child. Do not go through this alone. You need a support network of family, friends and others while you work through your grief. Eventually, you will move forward and start to focus on creating a new future for your child and yourself.

Highlights

- Take care of yourself and ask for help.
- Carve out quality time with your spouse.
- Avoid playing the blame game, and remember, not everyone grieves in the same way.
- Create family-centered solutions to cope with the impact of the disability.
- Educate your extended family about your child's disability and let them know how they can help.
- Maintain your social connections by reaching out.
- Build a support network.
- Seek out opportunities to meet other mothers of children with disabilities so you don't feel so isolated and alone. Learn from their experiences.
- Find reliable sources of information about your child's disability and learn the best practices to help them succeed.

Getting Ready

- Research information to become familiar with your child's disability.

- Make a list of places in your area or online that you can meet other mothers of children with disabilities.

- Identify the existing people in your support network. Then determine if you have unmet needs and come up with a plan on how to increase your circle of support.

Magers and Spencer

Chapter 2

....

Planning for the Future

By failing to prepare you are preparing to fail.
-- Benjamin Franklin

The day-to-day activities of raising a child with a disability are demanding and time consuming, and it may seem that it is all you can do. But in no time at all your child will be finished with school and heading out into the adult world. You must prepare for that day now. So before getting into the nitty gritty we suggest taking a step back to get a larger perspective and looking at the big picture.

Assessing Your Child

It is important to have high expectations for your child's future while keeping in mind his or her wishes and dreams. Ask yourself these questions:

- What does my child do well?
- When does my child struggle?

33

- What are my child's interests and passions?
- What are my child's talents?
- What skills are needed for my child to be ready to participate in post-secondary education, to hold down a job, and to live independently?
- Where does the focus need to be in school, at home and in the community to make sure my child has the best life possible?

If your child has more significant disabilities the questions become more challenging:

- Who will take care of my child if I can't?
- Will a guardian or personal care assistant be needed to make decisions and look out for my child's interests?
- What type of housing will be available?
- How will I be able to pay for housing and personal care?

Asking these questions now, even if you don't have immediate answers for some of them, will provide you with an overview and the extent of your challenges. That way you can at least start thinking about how to solve them over time.

Talk with school staff, a financial planner and an elder law attorney to help you learn more about these issues so you can make informed choices.

Challenges

When children have disabilities, we often dwell on what they can't do, ignoring what they can accomplish. School teams are especially guilty of focusing on the child's challenges instead of promoting their strengths. We can't ignore the deficits, but spending time discovering strengths and interests can be much more productive.

Ben's Story

Many students struggle with finding out what they want to do. They float. For example, Ben skipped school more than he attended. He ended up in a photography class because the computer class his mother wanted him to take was full. When he told her what had happened, she wanted to demand of the school that he be placed in the computer class. Luckily, she listened to Ben when he begged her not to interfere. He told her that it was the first class that he had taken that he loved. He graduated from high school, attended a school that focused specifically on photography, and became a successful commercial photographer.

Strengths

Discovering your child's strengths involves listening, asking questions about preferences and feelings, and observing how your child responds and acts in a variety of settings. Record your observations in a journal. Also include information about your child's personal wishes and dreams, behavioral tendencies, quirks, personality traits and frustrations. Sharing this information with your school team and brainstorming how to use it to help your child master the goals in the Individual Education Plan (IEP) can be very productive.

This process of discovering your child's strengths can make planning for the future much easier. It also teaches your child the valuable skill of self-discovery.

Marjorie's Story

Marjorie did not know what she wanted to do after high school. She had an opportunity to visit the local technical school and shadow a few of its programs. The Veterinarian Tech program seemed like it might be a good fit because she loved animals, but during her visit she realized the focus was on working with farm animals rather than cats and dogs. Although the llamas and cows were cute, Marjorie had no desire to be around large, smelly animals. She also discovered that she did not like being outside in the heat.

Marjorie's other interest was in art. Her job coach suggested they take a look at a digital design course. The teacher warmly greeted Marjorie when she walked into the room, gave her an overview of the types of things she would learn in the class, and talked about the different kinds of jobs available to people with graphic design skills. It sounded like an exciting opportunity to Marjorie. Prior to her visit, she had never even heard of the graphic design field, but now she decided to sign up for the course.

It would take two years to complete the program, so Marjorie met with her IEP team at school to discuss her options. They decided she should break her senior year into two parts, which would allow her to graduate from high school with a standard diploma and with industry certifications in the graphic design software programs. The course was an excellent fit for Marjorie and she discovered she really liked digital design. She could now see the possibility of having a promising career.

Exposure to opportunities, especially for children with disabilities, gives them a broader view of the world. It also helps them figure out where they can use their talents and interests in a productive way.

What does the future hold?

This brings us to the process that schools use to help you plan for your child's future; the Individual Education Plan (IEP). We will discuss IEP meetings in detail in a later chapter. For now we just want to look at how the plan figures in your approach to your child's future in later life.

It turns out that IEP goals are written for only one year at a time. That's why you need to be the one who thinks farther ahead. Each year helps determine where your child will be when it is time to leave school. In the early years, your child's IEP goals might focus on improving communication or learning how to follow the rules in a classroom. Another goal might concentrate on developing fine motor skills needed to hold a pencil. These essential skills are required when your child becomes an adult.

To live independently, a person must be able to communicate with others in the community. Employers expect company rules to be followed. Success in college or trade school depends on good writing and typing skills. There is an important connection between early goals and the skills children will need as adults.

Each time the IEP team arrives at a decision point, the choices you make will affect where your child will end up in the future. You may be asked to decide whether or not your child will participate in standardized testing or access a modified curriculum. If you think a modified curriculum is appropriate, find out what that means regarding your child's ability to earn a standard high school diploma. If your child receives a special diploma, will it limit his or her ability to attend post-secondary education or to get a certain job? There are not right or wrong answers to these questions, but the choices you make may significantly influence opportunities your child will have in the future.

The school setting offers many chances to help prepare your child for the future in a safe and supported environment. Take advantage of these opportunities by letting your child attend IEP meetings even if participation is limited to just the introductory portion of the meeting.

As your child gets older, he or she may stay in the meeting for longer periods of time and begin to participate in the process of developing goals. Upon reaching their sixteenth birthday, children must be invited to attend their IEP meetings by law. The team will expect them to give input into their annual goals and will ask probing questions about their plans after they leave school.

The school team has the responsibility of helping children learn self-advocacy skills and allowing them to exercise self-determination. You can help your child develop these skills by encouraging choices. Ask your child the following questions: Where do you want to go to dinner? Which color shirt do you prefer? Which movie would you like to see? Making such decisions and choices can be difficult, so your child needs to practice in order to learn how to speak up.

The following story illustrates the importance of how early decisions may impact your child's future.

Marcy's Story

Marcy has autism. At four-years-old, she started school in a special education preschool class. The class had a teacher, an aide and eight children. Marcy's progress amazed her mother. The next year, the school decided to offer a similar kindergarten setting.

During Marcy's kindergarten year, her parents had her evaluated at the multi-disciplinary center of their local university. The team of professionals consisted of an occupational therapist, a speech-language pathologist, an educator and a developmental pediatrician. The team spent three days talking with Marcy's mom, observing Marcy and performing various evaluations. At the end of the process, the team presented a comprehensive report of Marcy's strengths, challenges and a recommendation for school placement.

The evaluations showed that Marcy struggled with communication and social interactions. However, reading and comprehension scores were above grade level and she demonstrated other strong academic skills. The team felt that, with appropriate supports and services, Marcy would be able to go to school with her peers in a regular education classroom, and succeed with the standard curriculum.

The proposed changes terrified Marcy's mom. Her daughter received a lot of individualized attention in the small, special education class. She had difficulty understanding why a move to a class with twenty students would be a better placement. The educator on the team explained, "We don't have a special world for children with disabilities."

After considering the educator's perspective about being in a separate class and how it could impact Marcy's future, the mom realized that even though initially it would be harder for Marcy to be in the bigger class, in the long run she would be better off and more prepared to live as an independent adult.

The school called an IEP meeting to plan for first grade. They were surprised when Marcy's mom presented them with the multi-disciplinary evaluations and requested placement in regular education. At the recommendation of the university team, she also asked for Marcy to have aide support in the classroom. The school team said it needed to consult with staff at the district office to consider her request.

After the meeting one of the school staff members pulled mom aside and told her to stick to her guns and not back down from her requests. The school staff agreed that Marcy needed to be in a regular education classroom with support, but had been told to keep quiet because the school did not have the resources to provide an aide. The staff member said, "I've seen mothers move mountains and you can too."

Marcy went to first grade with aide support. There were some rocky moments, but she made it through.

Fast forward… Marcy graduated with a 3.95 GPA and earned a standard diploma from her districted high school.

Highlights

- Offer your child encouragement and opportunities to explore interests and passions.
- Embrace your child's dreams rather than trying to impose your own.
- Focus on the positive and what your child can do.
- Identify the skills your child will need to be ready to participate in post-secondary education, to have a job and to live independently.
- Provide opportunities for your child to experience post-secondary and career options first-hand.
- Know decisions you make each year will affect your child's future.

Getting Ready

- Write a list of 10 positive things about your child.

- Start a discovery journal about your child and record your observations, insights, works samples, etc.

- If you have a child in middle or high school, make a list of post-secondary schools and employers that your child could visit to start exploring life after school. Work with the school to setup opportunities to see programs that your child has expressed an interest in.

- Select a piece of paper that you will keep in your record keeping binder. Write down your child's current age and your vision for the future when your child is 25. Include work, housing, transportation, leisure activities, and friendships. List the skills, talents and interests that your child must develop that will make your dream come true. Include barriers and how to overcome them. Detail what can be worked on now to insure your child's success in the future. Prior to each IEP meeting do this same exercise and compare your answers over time.

- If you have a child with a more significant disability, locate a financial planner and an elder law attorney who specialize in support plans for people with disabilities. Start working on the "what if" plan so you know your child will be taken care of if you are no longer able to do so.

Chapter 3

Acting as Project Manager

No matter what the work you are doing,
be always ready to drop it. And plan it,
so as to be able to leave it.

—Leo Tolstoy

As if you don't have enough to do, we are assigning you a new job. Congratulations on becoming the Project Manager on your child's IEP team!

When a child becomes eligible for special education services, a team comes together to develop an Individual Education Plan (IEP). The federal law that governs special education, the Individuals with Disabilities Education Improvement Act of 2004 (IDEA), requires that, at a minimum, the team members must consist of the child's special education teacher, a general education teacher, a Local Education Agency (LEA) representative and the parent.

School team members tend to focus on making sure that they are in compliance with the law while the parent's focus is on the best interest of the child.

The mom's role, however, goes beyond just being a team member. First, you are the one who sees the big picture. You know your child's medical and emotional history, as well as your family dynamics. This perspective gives you the broad overview none of the others have. And that, above all, qualifies you to be the project manager.

It will become your job to know who the IEP team members are and what roles they play. You will become a good record keeper, a researcher, a progress monitor, and a communication facilitator. You will be the one who keeps all the pertinent information in one place and the one who follows up to make sure promises are fulfilled.

At this point, you may be feeling totally overwhelmed. We understand. But don't throw your hands up in despair quite yet. After all, you have already developed managerial skills by running your own household. Your child's success in school is crucial, and who better to advocate for him or her than you. Besides, we will share techniques, tools and resources we discovered in our own efforts to make sure that our children's educational needs were met. Don't become discouraged. It takes time to learn new skills.

Know the Team

As a first step, we recommend you make a list of everyone on your child's IEP team. Your contact person at the school, usually your child's teacher, should be able to give you this list. You will need the team member's name, title, role they play on the team, and their contact information.

If possible, establish more personal relationships with the key players such as the special education teacher and the general education teacher. Building rapport and trust outside the IEP meeting makes it easier to work together to put a solid plan in place for your child.

Research

Learn all you can about the IEP process and how it will relate to your child's disability. The Internet has a ton of information at your fingertips but make sure to use only reliable sources. Start with nationally recognized disability organizations and university based websites. Parent blogs and sites can help you connect with others who are having similar experiences but recognize the information they are providing is often an opinion or an anecdotal report on their child and not research-based, scientific facts. Talk to other moms who have older children with disabilities and learn from their experiences.

Keep Records

Some of you are saying right now, "But the school keeps a file on every child. Why should I keep my own records?" You are right, schools do that, but remember, they are bureaucratic organizations that serve many people. We know of too many cases in which documents have been misfiled, discarded or simply lost, never to be seen again. So do not rely on the school to keep track of your child's records; this is part of your job as the educational project manager. By keeping everything organized and in one place, you can easily access the information as you plan for your child's next IEP.

Facilitate Communication

Most school teams communicate via email. Make sure your team has your email address and puts you on the distribution list when they send out information regarding your child. If you do not have access to the Internet, let the school team know the best way to reach you and when you will be available.

Often, teachers have a difficult time taking phone calls during the school day. If you feel the need to speak with your child's teacher, send an email or note in advance to schedule a time to either meet or talk on the phone. A planned meeting time gives both parties a chance to collect their thoughts and come prepared to the discussion.

Monitor Progress

All IEPs need to be monitored to make sure that the plan is being implemented as written, and that your child is making measurable progress towards attaining the goals agreed upon. The team must send you progress notes at least quarterly with your child's report card. Your job will be to look for and review the progress reports, follow up with the team on a regular basis to make sure things are going well, and, if they are not, ask to reconvene the IEP team.

Follow Up

Any time your interaction with the school team results in a decision or an agreement to take an action, you should follow up with an email recapping the discussion. For example, if you talk with your child's teacher and agree that they will get together during lunch once week to review words prior to the spelling test, then you should send an email to the teacher afterward, outlining the agreement. That way you will have a paper trail. You will find out soon enough, if not here in these pages, then from your own experience, how important that is.

Organization System

Purchase a three-ring binder. Once your child enters the school system, you will be inundated with papers—meeting notices, activity fliers, graded papers, and more. The list goes on and on. Having a child with a disability is likely to result in your pile of paper doubling. Much of the IEP-related paperwork is very important to keep for the future.

We suggest keeping your child's finished and graded school work in a basket or container until you receive a progress report or report card. This makes it easy to check that the grades match up and allow you to follow up with the teacher if you spot an error.

Important education records, such as IEPs, evaluations, doctor's reports, meeting notices, etc. should be put in your three-ring binder with easy access in mind. Sort your papers in reverse chronological order—the most recent first. Typically, you will be referring to the most current information so you want it on top. Never give away or write with ink or colored highlighters on an original document. Make notations in pencil, if you must, or use sticky notes.

You should also keep correspondence with the school in your binder. When working with the public schools or any agency, your experience will be better if you have a written record of all communications with that organization. Letters, emails and reports should go in your binder. Keep a telephone-log with a summary of all conversations. It should include the name of the person/persons you talked to, the date and time, and an account of all conclusions, decisions and actions taken. Even conversations with the staff in the hallway should be documented.

Other supplies we find helpful to use in the binder are:

- Sheet protectors to hold work samples or any papers that you don't want to hole punch
- Business card holder sheets for your contact information
- Removable tabs to label important documents for quick reference

If you think this is excessive, we can tell you it is not. Much of the IEP-related paperwork is very important, and can prove essential in the future.

Tommy's Story

Tommy has severe autism. He was assigned to a specially designed class for children with Autism Spectrum Disorder (ASD) but the teacher of the class was a long-term substitute without special education training. As a result, he was losing skills rather than gaining them and his behavior deteriorated at an alarming rate.

Tommy's mom was extremely organized. She worked in a job that required her to maintain patient's health records. Having data and documentation accurate and complete could mean life or death for a patient. Tommy's mom applied the same practice to maintaining his school records.

She setup a binder with all of the data from the school in reverse chronological order. The IEP required the teacher to provide daily reports on Tommy's behavior and his skill acquisition. She also received weekly reports from his speech-language and occupational therapists. As she reviewed the information, it was obvious that Tommy was struggling and getting worse as the weeks went on. She called several meetings with the school, but nothing was

resolved. The school claimed they could not find a qualified, permanent teacher.

Finally, Tommy's parents had enough and they filed a
due process complaint but they agreed to a mediation meeting to try and work out a solution. Nobody really wanted to
go to court.

Tommy's mom wrote up a statement of the points she
wanted to make in the meeting about how the IEP was not
being followed. She also organized a notebook with evidence
to support each point that she planned to make. During
the meeting, with each statement she made, she handed the
exceptional student education director a packet of information to support her claim. By the end of her remarks, without any deliberation, the director asked her what it would
take to make her happy.

Tommy's mom asked for a change of schools to an established autism program that had an excellent teacher.
She also wanted the district to pay for her transportation
costs—driving 60 miles a day to and from the school—
and that her daughter also be transferred so that both
children could attend the same school. She got everything
she asked for because her documentation was in order
and she could prove her points. Tommy made significant
progress in his new school and the parent and school staff
maintained their relationship.

We cannot emphasize enough how important it is to put everything in writing. As far as bureaucracies are concerned, if it is
not written down, it did not happen. Every interaction you have
with the school including phone calls, parent conferences, and
even conversations in the hallway should be documented. This may
seem tedious, but is very necessary.

Katie's Story

Recently, we worked with a family whose daughter, Katie, was in a charter school. Katie was struggling with reading and her family suspected she had a learning disability. Katie's mom met with the school team and requested they evaluate her daughter to see if she had a disability. The team agreed and had mom sign a consent form. The consent form is very important, because the day you sign the form starts the clock ticking on how soon the school must complete the evaluation in order to be in compliance with the law.

The school also told Katie's mom that it was behind on getting kids tested and did not have a lot of money to do this kind of testing. It would be much faster if she moved Katie back to her regular district school. (This is not legal or ethical! Charter schools are public schools and they have a responsibility to test their students, but that is another subject...)

Katie's mom agreed to move schools as long as the charter school principal would call the receiving school and update the staff there on Katie's academic progress, tell them about her need for evaluation, and send over the consent form. The principal did all of those things and Katie's mom made notes and kept copies of all of the documents.

Katie started at the new school and a few months went by. Her mom called to find out when the testing would be completed, and was shocked to find out that no one at the school had any idea what she was talking about. They invited her to a meeting where the team agreed to do the testing but asked Katie's mom to sign another consent form because they did not have the original. When she said, "I will sign it, but I have a copy of the original," they told her that having a copy of the original did not matter and that they now had another sixty days to finish testing from the date of the second consent form.

This infuriated Katie's mom, but she kept control of her emotions and decided on the next step. She called the district office, explained the story, and faxed both forms. The district coordinator contacted the school, bumped Katie to the top of the testing list and within three weeks Katie had an IEP in place.

Moral of the story: Having a copy of the original signed consent form and notes about the conversations between the schools put Katie's mom in a position of power because she could prove her case and she had the law on her side. Write it down and save all documents.

You can keep older documents that need to be saved in file folders and put them in a box where they can still be found quickly. That way you don't have to carry them with you to meetings.

School Records

The Family Educational Rights and Privacy Act (FERPA), a federal law, protects the privacy of students and parents. It also gives parents the right to inspect their child's educational records, to receive copies of the documents for a reasonable fee, and to have school staff explain the content in detail. It further outlines procedures for having records amended if the information is not correct.

FERPA also provides guidelines on who may review your child's educational records and when permission to do so is needed. Generally, parents must give written consent before information that identifies their child personally can be disclosed. In some cases, such as an internal audit or in response to a subpoena, information may be released without your consent, but the school must keep a log of all such disclosures.

We recommend that you review your child's educational records every few years. People who have had no prior contact with your child will get their first impression of his or her abilities from the information contained in the cumulative record, also known as the "Cum" file. You will want to make sure that these records are complete and accurate. Again, don't assume that schools, which have to process massive amounts of paper, can be relied on not to make mistakes, misfile or even lose essential documents.

Guidelines for Reviewing School Cumulative Files

We recommend that you review your child's file at the end of second grade, fifth grade, eighth grade and eleventh grade. Any time your child moves to a different school make sure to review the file then as well.

Always request a monitored review. This means a school staff member will be present while you go through the file to witness your actions and answer questions. You do not ever want to be in the position of being accused of adding or removing something from the file. We're not suggesting that schools go out of their way to attribute such misconduct to parents, but it has happened.

Take along sticky notes or flags to mark any pages you may want to have for your own records. At the end of the review notify the staff member that you need copies made and find out when you can pick them up. Some schools will make copies while you wait, others will schedule a date for pick up. You may be charged a reasonable fee for the copies.

Highlights

- Embrace the role of project manager. This includes establishing a good line of communication with the school, making sure that the IEP is being followed and ensuring that your child is making progress.

- Develop a filing system that works for you.

- Maintain the system on a regular basis so you don't get overwhelmed.

- Organize your documentation so you have evidence to support your position.

- Write it down. If it isn't written down, it did not happen.

- Review your files annually and archive anything that is no longer relevant.

- Make an appointment with the school every few years to review your child's cumulative record.

Getting Ready

1. Make a contact list of people in your school system including their email addresses and phone numbers. It is always better to do this when you are not in a crisis. The list should include:

   - School Board Members
   - Superintendent
   - Special Education Department Director
   - Principal of your child's school
   - Assistant Principals
   - School-based Special Education compliance person
   - Guidance Counselor
   - Your child's teachers (remember to get contact information for art, music, physical education, etc...)

2. Set up your organizational system and binder. (See Appendix A—"Getting Organized" for a more detailed list, including and example of a follow-up letter to create a paper trail.)

3. At the beginning of each school year, create a new binder.

Chapter 4

Becoming a Problem Solver

Your biggest enemy is the unknown and assumptions.
—Lieutenant General Claude Christianson

One of the most important skills needed in dealing with school personnel is problem solving. In your regular job as a mother, you are probably used to solving a myriad of big and small problems every day already. Working with the school on your child's behalf will allow you to put those skills to use in another setting.

In addition, if you haven't already, you may need to develop others, such as the ability to communicate successfully with your education partners, keep your emotions in check, behave in a professional manner, ask the right questions, and identify an acceptable outcome to resolve the issue.

Communicating in Person

Being an effective part of a team requires you to be able to communicate in a manner that conveys your desires while allowing the other members to be open and honest so you can put together a plan for your child's education. An assertive, clear communication style helps. What does it take to do that? Be an active listener; check on the feelings of others on the team while stating your expectations and limits. Behave non-judgmentally, confidently, and realistically. Be aware of your body language—strive to maintain eye contact and avoid a defensive posture.

You may get to a place in a meeting that you disagree with the team. Calmly explain your objections by stating facts rather than attacking people. If you do not understand what someone said, ask for clarification.

You will find it easier to communicate assertively if you are prepared for the meeting and know your desired outcome in advance. Jot down notes about what you want to say and highlight for yourself any important points you want to make about your child's needs. When you talk to people in a calm and confident manner, they are more likely to want to work with you and your child.

Natalie's Story

Natalie's son, Doug, was brilliant and had been placed in a gifted and talented program. His math skills were off the chart but his ability to understand verbal instruction and organize his work was poor. He was a visual learner and had great difficulty taking notes in class. Natalie helped him schedule his time effectively with calendars and charts and she broke down assignments for him. She knew that if she could get assignments and course expectations in advance she could be even more effective when scheduling his work. So she asked each of Doug's teachers to provide her with a syllabus for their class.

This request upset some of the teachers who did not have one or didn't understand what a syllabus is. Natalie knew that in colleges and universities professors provided a syllabus at the beginning of a course, which contained specific information about the class, outlined objectives, and included a schedule of when assignments were due and when exams would be given. This information allowed a student to plan ahead. She never imagined that such a simple request would trigger such outrage in the high school?

An administrator was called in to mediate the problem. During the meeting it became embarrassingly obvious that he did not know, or chose to act like he didn't know, what a syllabus was and why it was needed. He actually stood up, grabbed a phone book off a shelf, threw it on the floor and then screamed, "What do you expect teachers to do? Write a book?"

Natalie stood up as well and calmly defined the term syllabus and explained why she wanted one. She pointed out that it didn't need to be lengthy but needed to let Doug know when assignments were due and when exams would take place. She didn't call the administrator on his bizarre behavior and continued to request what she wanted in a calm but firm voice.

End of story, Natalie got what she wanted. Doug graduated from high school and was accepted at a major university where he has been very successful.

The upshot of this story is that it behooves parents to always act in a professional manner. This statement may seem odd. We expect people in positions of power, especially teachers and administrators, to behave that way; but sometimes they don't. You, on the other hand, if you want to resolve problems and get things done, always need to maintain your professionalism when you work with your school team.

Communicating in Writing

In many cases, difficulties can be better resolved by written contact by letter or email. It works well because it allows you to clarify what you wish to say and gives the other party time to consider and formulate a reasoned response. Furthermore, it leaves a distinct paper trail documenting clearly what issues need to be addressed.

Here are some guidelines. Each piece of communication needs to have a purpose and should include a request for a written reply. If there are multiple issues, bullet point the correspondence to make it easier to read and understand. This will make it more likely that your concerns receive a fair hearing.

The cardinal rule of writing is: Be clear and succinct in your communication. Less is more. Long letters detailing every slight, hurt or painful interaction may cause the recipient's eyes to roll or, even worse, to glaze over. We once advised a parent to put her concerns in writing and were surprised and dismayed when she sent a six-page letter to the principal of the school, the administrators at the district office, and the school board members. The response she got as a result did not help her get the assistance she needed for her child.

Zeroing in on the problem and suggesting or requesting possible solutions certainly takes thought and clarity. In the midst of an emotional situation you may want to vent. If that helps you, fine. Just don't send your first draft. Having someone else read what you have written can help eliminate unneeded or unclear wording.

Problem Solving Steps

When dealing with any challenge, it helps to collect your thoughts and take a logical approach to resolving the issue.

Step 1. Get your emotions in check! When your child has a problem in school you may get mad at your child or the teacher depending on whose story you get first. Refrain from acting based on that feeling!

Step 2. Get out your magnifying glass and start collecting clues to figure out what really happened. Talk to your child and get his or her version of the story. Then call or email the teacher to see if there is another point of view. If you are using email, be aware that your tone may be misread. Avoid making accusations. Report the facts as you know them and ask probing questions. Remember, your child will probably continue to go to this person's classroom every day.

Step 3. Document everything you do. Keep a log of phone calls and include when, who was involved, and what was said. Follow up with an email to thank the other party for being helpful and clarify your understanding of what was said and agreed to be done. **If it isn't written down, it did not happen.**

Step 4. Once you have gathered information by talking to the people involved, decide what a "win" looks like for your child. **Know what you want**. You can't resolve an issue if you don't know what will satisfy you in a situation. If someone from the school says to you directly, "What do you want us to do about...," you better have an answer to that question.

Step 5. Know when to cut your losses. Sometimes you can act in good faith and try diligently to be a good partner with the school and still fail to come to agreement on a solution to a problem. For big issues that will greatly affect your child, you may even need to consider changing teachers or changing schools. Think about all of your options and make a decision you feel works best for your child. Try not to let your feelings get in the way of making a logical decision. If you are too emotional about the situation, let some time pass and talk to someone further removed from the conflict before you take an action you may regret.

In fact, it is a good idea to think before taking action in all situations. Ask yourself: Do I need to elevate the conversation or tone it down? Should I just document what happened? Should I do nothing? Figuring out what action to take can be the hard part, and you will learn as you go. Sometimes doing nothing for the moment gives you time to plan your strategy and your next step. But you also need to know when to take action. Remember, your child's safety always comes first!

Once your child enters the school system and needs special education services, you will face ongoing challenges. Keep a level head, try to set emotions aside and stick with the facts. Find the people who are allies and can help you develop a solution designed to provide positive results for your child. The following worksheet outlines a formula for problem solving.

Formula for Problem Solving

1. Define the problem. What is really wrong?
2. Why do you think the problem happened? This is your guess, so be prepared to find out that you may

be missing a few facts. Proceed with caution so you do not create enemies as you gather information.

3. Who can help you solve the problem?

4. What limitations does that person have in being part of the solution?

5. What rules, policies, or laws caused the problem or may impact your choice of solutions?

6. Identify what you want as a resolution to the problem, but be flexible in case new information is revealed that may change the desired outcome.

Gretchen's Story

Let us tell you about the most difficult parent meeting we ever attended.

In third grade, Gretchen had a terrible teacher. Everyone in the school knew this teacher was a terror. Her classroom management style was to scream at the children and to use ridicule to help them learn. Unfortunately, she had been in the school for a long time and the administration would not do anything to get rid of her.

Throughout the first half of the year the situation became worse and worse for Gretchen. There was nothing she could do to make the teacher happy. When her mother tried meeting with the teacher, it only compounded the problem. Apparently, the teacher did not care for Gretchen's mother any more than she liked Gretchen. The child came home with severe stomach aches, started having bathroom accidents in school, and was totally stressed out. Her parents were beside themselves. They took her to a doctor who examined her and told them to get her out of that situation.

At that point, the family made an appointment with the principal of the school, even though he had a strict rule that he would not consider a class change for any reason. Other moms on campus warned the family that the meeting would be very difficult, that the principal would show very little compassion and probably defend the teacher. The parents called on us at the last minute to go with them to the meeting.

We had a brief planning strategy session just before the meeting and asked the parents:

What outcome do you desire from the meeting?

What are your non-negotiable items?

What can you bargain with that is really not important, but can let the principal feel like he won something?

The parents were in such a distressed emotional state that they had a difficult time developing a coherent strategy. Other than wanting a different teacher, they could not define what was needed to help their child.

We went into the meeting and it was as ugly as we had feared. The principal blamed the parents and the child and suggested that they could move to another school. He had brought along other staff members to support his positions. The mom cried and the dad got mad, and the principal finally agreed to change the class. But the solution turned out to be worse than the problem. The class he insisted Gretchen be moved to had the one teacher on campus that was worse than the teacher she already had. We tried to talk him out of this decision but he would not be swayed. He was a very passive-aggressive man.

Gretchen attended the new class for two days and became so sick that her parents pulled her out and home schooled her for the rest of the year. She never returned to this school and the parents are still angry.

What might the parents have done differently in this situation? Gretchen's mom would have started out by documenting every time her daughter came home upset and would have communicated with the teacher via email to try and resolve the problem. If the child continued to have difficulty in the class, she would have scheduled a meeting with the teacher and asked that the assistant principal attend to help facilitate a resolution that would make the situation better for the child. If that still did not work, she would have asked the assistant principal to schedule a meeting with the principal to get a class change. Since the assistant principal was already invested in solving the problem, more than likely she would have been an ally in the meeting with the principal.

After hearing from so many parents about how difficult this principal was going to be about making the class change, she would also have invited someone from the district office to attend the meeting. Having an administrator present who does not report to the principal, but works within the system, can help to bring a different perspective to a meeting. When you invite someone from outside the building you build in accountability for the staff.

Gretchen's mom would have done some research prior to the meeting to find out about the other teachers in the grade, since there was another teacher who was obviously not a good fit, and would not improve the situation. She would have addressed that issue early in the meeting in order to remove that person as a potential solution to the problem.

Before you walk into a meeting, you must know what you want and don't want. Figure out a strategy by gathering facts, aligning allies and staying focused on the desired outcome for your child.

Highlights

- Use an assertive communication style.
- Be clear and succinct in your communication.
- Always behave in a professional manner.
- Document everything. If it isn't written down, it didn't happen.
- Keep your emotions in check. Think before taking action in all situations.

Getting Ready

- Write down the six Steps to Problem Solving in the front of your binder.
- Also recreate the Formula for Problem Solving worksheet to use as a guide to help you work through a crisis without responding from a place of emotion.
- Get to know the staff in your child's school. Take time to meet your child's teacher(s), guidance counselor, special education staff, and administrators. Making this investment up front can have huge payoffs if something goes wrong because you have already established relationships.

Chapter 5

Navigating the School System

The time to repair the roof is when the sun is shining.
-- John F. Kennedy

When advocating for their child at a particular school, parents often feel that they can't get to the right person or that they are being given the run around. Part of the difficulty is systemic. The individual school and its personnel are part of a larger district with a host of intermediaries and decision makers. It helps to understand the complexity of the larger school system. This will allow you to be more effective, save time, and get the support your child needs.

The good news is that there are a many excellent people working for the school district who want your child to succeed. Once you can come to agreement on the specifics of the programs and support, the public school system often provides the most talented teachers and therapists, and the best curriculum and equipment to allow your child to be educated appropriately and make progress. Remember, the school system belongs to the community and entitles your child to a Free Appropriate Public Education (FAPE).

School systems operate based on rules, regulations, policies and procedures designed to handle efficiently the large number of people using services. As a result, it can be challenging to know the right person to solve a problem. However, taking time to learn the system and develop relationships will pay off. You should never underestimate the value of knowing the "right people" to go to in order to get things put in place for your child. When it comes to dealing with the public school system to get the optimal support for your child, you need to know two things:

1. How it is set up and
2. Who is in charge.

Let's deal with the system first

Most school districts have two parts—an elected school board and an elected or appointed superintendent. A school board writes policy, makes financial decisions, and approves personnel decisions for the district. The superintendent manages daily operations of the schools. Everyone who works in the school district ultimately reports to the superintendent.

Depending on the size of your school district, there may be multiple layers of administrators and specialists at the district central office. If you live in a small school district, the relationship between the school principals and the superintendent may be more direct.

Parents and community members can have input and affect change at the district level by talking with school board members or by speaking at school board meetings. At some point, you may feel the need to be involved at the district level, but most parents focus their advocacy at the school where their child attends.

At the local school, the principal assigns teachers to their specific jobs, decides what class a child will be placed in, chooses the curriculum that will be used in the school, has responsibility for oversight of the school budget, and implements the school improvement plan. You will need the support of the principal to allocate resources if your child needs something special to be successful.

Everyone that comes in contact with your child in the school system should be working in your child's best interest. However, keep in mind that school staff has the responsibility for providing an appropriate education to all children while your primary responsibility rests with your child.

Charter Schools and Private Schools

We would be remiss if we did not talk a bit about charter schools and private schools.

Charter schools are public schools that do not have to play by the same set of rules as a traditional public school. They are usually run by a management company or a local independent school board, and they offer something different than a traditional school. For example, they might focus on the arts or technology or a military themed curriculum. Charter schools have to accept students with disabilities, but the resources they have available to support them may be less than what you could find in a traditional public school. If you are considering a charter school, make sure to ask questions about the services outlined on your child's Individual Education Plan (IEP) and how those services will be delivered at the school. If your child has an IEP and attends a charter school, you retain all of your federal rights granted under the Individuals with Disability Improvement Act (IDEA).

Private schools, which are also known as independent schools, non-governmental, or nonstate schools, include religious based institutions and preparatory academies. Students who attend private schools may be able to receive some special education services paid for by federal funds. The local school district will meet with the private school operators to determine how much money is available and what types of services the private schools would like to purchase. Often, private schools use the money to make therapies available to their students with disabilities. This varies from district to district, so if you select a private school you should ask what is available to your child. A private school does not have to follow your child's IEP, and you do not have the same protections for your child as you would at a public school. The website *www.understandingspecialeducation.com/private-school.html* provides more information about services available to private school students.

Who's in Charge?

To work within a school system successfully you need to know the players, the policies and the politics. Roadblocks can usually be categorized as a policy issue, a procedural problem, or someone's opposing opinion. Being able to discern the underlying cause will empower you to solve the problem. Having knowledge gives you power.

Classroom teachers have the most influence on your child's educational experience. Therefore, you need to form positive relationships and have good lines of communication. A majority of your advocacy time will be spent working directly with your child's teacher(s).

Start by introducing yourself at the beginning of the school year. Make sure to tell the teacher those things that help your child be successful in school.

Follow-up with a short email saying that you are looking forward to working together and that you want to be a supportive parent and partner in the education process. If you have a special talent or want to volunteer at the school, this would be a good time to share that. Ask the teacher the best way to communicate and provide your contact information and availability.

Create a brief one-page overview of your child's strengths, interests and needs and send it along as an attachment. Most likely your child already has an IEP which the teacher will follow in order to provide instruction and monitor progress. Any specific information you can offer about what has or has not worked in the past will usually be welcomed.

If your child has more than one teacher, repeat the process with all of them.

Get to Know All the Players

Being on good terms with your child's teacher is essential, but not enough. You must branch out. Get to know the members of your child's school team on a professional basis. Take their business cards and ask about their experience in working with children with disabilities. Talk with other parents and staff. Learn about the culture at your school and in your district. Did the superintendent rise from the teaching ranks or come from another place? Find out where most decisions are made—by teachers, by the principal or at the district level?

Chain of Command

Chain of Command refers to the order of authority or power in an organization. Ignoring the chain of command can ruin a relationship with a teacher. If a concern arises with your child, always start with the person closest to the problem. If you encounter a problem when working with the school you will need to be able to support your position with data and show that you attempted to work from the ground up to find a solution. This means that if your child has a problem in art class, talk to the art teacher first. Don't go over her head directly to the principal or call a school board member. Why? Because every person in the district is trained to ask the question, "Did you speak with the art teacher about this problem and try to work it out?" If you answer no, the person may not be willing to help you.

If you cannot find common ground with the teacher, your next step would be to talk to the immediate supervisor, then the principal. Continue to work your way up the chain until you can fix the problem or decide you need a more formal method of conflict resolution. Methodically working your way through the chain of command will give you a much stronger case to support your position.

Sometimes a problem may have developed because of a lack of resources. Teachers or staff cannot initiate a conversation to resolve this type of issue. But, after you have talked with the teacher, you can go to the next level to obtain the resources or services that your child needs.

Determine who the final decision-makers are by talking with teachers and other parents. Take time to build relationships and figure out who will be your allies in future negotiations.

Sophie's Story

Sophie's son was struggling with organizational skills which caused him to not have the information he needed to complete his homework at night. The school had put a plan in place to solve the problem but it was not working.

Sophie had met with all the relevant teachers and administrators at the school, and they were either not willing or unable to solve the problem. Sophie knew who to talk to at the district office about this issue. She met with the Executive Director of Exceptional Student Education and her staff.

At first, they told her that this was a school based issue and that the district office would not intervene. However, Sophie had documented all the meetings she had with the school staff and could show that their interventions had not worked.

The thorough documentation alerted the Executive Director to the fact that Sophie would be able to file a State Complaint to get the problem resolved unless the school district took action. The Executive Director further realized that the district would not be successful in proving the student was getting an appropriate education.

Sophie made it very clear that she did not want to fight a legal battle but needed someone to step in so that her son could receive an appropriate education. The Executive Director and her staff met with the school administrators and explained what they needed to do. The team worked together to modify Sophie's son's schedule and put him in classes with teachers who understood how to work with his strengths and support his weaknesses.

Getting to the right person and being able to show that you have followed the chain of command makes it more likely that you can get support to solve the problem.

There are exceptions to following the chain of command. School needs to be a safe place for your child. Physical or emotional abuse cannot be tolerated. Immediately, report safety issues directly to the principal.

There is another wrinkle to dealing the decision makers in order to succeed with your plans for your child. Understanding a person's motivation, when making decisions, can help you to know what your next move should be in a meeting. It may be related to the emotional makeup of the player, the politics of the situation, or the policies generally operating in a district.

Madeleine's Story

Madeleine, an elementary age student, had a potentially life threatening heart condition, which required having a paraprofessional by her side with an automatic external defibrillator (AED) in case her heart stopped beating.

All Madeleine wanted was to fit in with her peers and be "normal." All her parents wanted was for her to be happy, safe at school and assured that the professionals in charge would know what to do if Madeleine got into distress and would be able to implement that plan, if necessary.

The school called a meeting with Madeleine's mother to develop a 504 Plan that would address Madeleine's medical issues. A 504 Plan provides accommodations or a health plan for a student with a disability so they can receive FAPE. The school personnel needed to work out the details of a crisis plan in case Madeleine had a health emergency.

Mom had worked well with the school in the past, so she was not particularly worried about getting everyone to agree on the details of the plan. Things were proceeding without a hitch until the school administrators informed her that they did not want the classroom teachers to call 911. Instead, they wanted the teachers to contact the school nurse or the front office staff and have them place the call. Madeleine's mother was shocked. When a child's heart stops beating, seconds matter, and you want emergency personnel on the way to the school as soon as possible. The school's reasoning did not make sense and she refused to finish the meeting and sign off on the plan.

The school called in district staff and county health department staff to try and come to agreement on who would make the 911 call, and when. The meeting notice Madeleine's parents received listed 25 people as attendees. This unusually large number alerted the family that the school district might be trying to intimidate them. Mom and dad decided both of them needed to go to the meeting. They also invited an advocate. Her role was to be an impartial listener and help figure out the players, policies and politics that would be driving the decision making.

Madeleine's mom brought a list of what she wanted the school to do and a written plan from her physician supporting her position. The meeting took about two hours and lots of people spoke about policies, procedures and whatnot. But, Madeleines' mom and dad stayed focused and stuck to their talking points.

At one point, the advocate was watching the face of the Special Education Department Director and saw her have an aha moment, when she realized that the parents were right. The advocate put a note in front of the mother to be quiet and let the Special Education Department Director talk. Knowing when to stop talking can be as important as knowing when to argue your point!

The Special Education Director got up, walked down to the principal and whispered in his ear. Suddenly, the meeting took a turn in another direction and the school decided to allow the teachers to call 911 from their cellphones and then put a call into the nurse and front office to apprise them of the situation. Madeleine got what she needed to be safe because we knew who the ultimate decision-maker was in the room and we were able to present information in a way that made that person an ally.

This story illustrates the importance of knowing who is in charge in the room, being familiar with the policies that govern the situation you are dealing with, and understanding the politics that may be influencing the decision-making.

Highlights

- Children with disabilities attending public schools and charter schools have the right to a free, appropriate public education and are protected by the individuals with Disabilities Education Improvement Act (IDEA).

- Children attending private schools do not have the protection of IDEA, the school does not have to follow the IEP, but there may be some special education services available.

- Cultivate a good relationship with your child's teacher(s).

- Know the chain of command.

- Find the right person to talk to about your problem.

- In meetings, know who is in charge of the room.

- Be familiar with the policies that govern the situation you are dealing with and understand the politics that may be influencing the decision-making.

- Have a written list of your important talking points and stay focused on your desired outcome.

Getting Ready

- Create a one-page summary/resume of your child's strengths, interests and needs, and share that with your child's teacher as an email attachment or hand deliver the document.

- Become familiar with the structure of your school district. Go to its website and see what type of resources and information are available for parents.

- Learn more about the culture in your school district by attending a school board meeting.

Chapter 6

Preparing for an IEP Meeting

Dreams are less influential than actions.
And actions are less influential than results.
—Bobby Darnell, football coach

As a mom advocating for your child, you will be going to a lot of meetings. In addition to the annual individual education program (IEP) meeting, you may be asked to attend meetings regarding eligibility for new programs, re-evaluations reviews, discontinuation of services, dismissal from a program and manifestation hearings.

Your school team will set up an IEP meeting to develop an education plan specifically designed to meet your child's needs that will allow them to benefit from the instruction provided in school. The team will also consider your child's future plans for post-secondary education, employment and independent living.

Be sure you know what kind of meeting you have been asked to attend and for what purpose. Knowing these things in advance will help you to be mentally prepared, have the right information and determine if you need to bring experts. If necessary, clarify the purpose of the meeting with your contact at school ahead of time.

Danielle's Story

Danielle was attending an IEP meeting with her husband and son. She thought they were there to talk about goals for her son's education for the following year. Instead the IEP team digressed and opened up a file folder that contained at least 10 note cards of Danielle's personal stationery. The notes were addressed to the school excusing absences. Danielle had not written the notes.

You guessed it: her son had enlisted several different girls to write them for him. He was embarrassed by being confronted in front of his parents and swore never to attend another IEP meeting again. Danielle's husband, who had taken time from work to attend the meeting, was disgusted and complained what a waste of time it had been. Danielle felt blindsided, too.

No IEP goals were written that day.

Prior to attending any meeting, ask the purpose of the meeting and for an outline or agenda of what will be covered. Try to eliminate surprises.

The Annual IEP Meeting

Perhaps the most important is the annual IEP meeting, which sets out the educational program and goals for your child for the coming school year. We have already mentioned that it is necessary for you to become the project manager of the IEP. In this chapter we want to discuss some of the major issues you're likely to encounter. Preparing properly for the meeting will allow you to feel more confident and be better able to represent your child's needs. Know how to be a member of the IEP Team!

Since IEP meetings are mandated by law, the school will send you an official notice that includes the time and date of the meeting, the purpose, and who will be attending. Your role will be to negotiate on your child's behalf to develop a program that meets your child's priority educational needs.

Members of the team will vary depending on your child's needs. Unless your child attends a separate special education day school, the team will always consist of a regular education teacher, a special education teacher and the local education agency representative (LEA). The LEA can commit district resources.

Although you must be invited to the meeting by law, you can decline to attend. In that case, the school staff can move forward without your participation. From what you have read so far, you know that your child needs you to be there to represent his or her interests. So, plan to attend. The school has to find a mutually convenient time and place to meet with you. You also have the option of participating by telephone or video conferencing.

You can bring anyone with you to the meeting who knows your child. This is a good thing. Take a spouse, significant other, relative, friend or advocate. We cannot say this too strongly:

DO NOT GO TO MEETINGS ALONE.

If your spouse goes to the meeting with you, make sure you are in accord. The last thing you want to do is argue or fight there with each other. Even if you don't totally agree, determine goals you can both live with before you meet with the rest of the team. You will be more effective advocates for your child if you deliver a united, consistent message to the school staff.

Other invitees to the meeting may be the school psychologist, social worker, guidance counselor, administrator, transition specialist, job coach, therapist, or outside agency providers. In fact, anyone whose services are needed to provide your child a *free appropriate public education* should be invited to the meeting. However, you want to try to keep the number of people as small as possible. Small groups work together better. You can always bring in other experts later, as they are needed.

Here are some other suggestions:

- **Get as much information as possible ahead of time.** School staff prepare in advance when developing an IEP. You will want to be just as prepared, so request copies of any reports or evaluations and take time before the meeting to examine them and analyze the data. This will help you set your priorities and give you time to sort your emotions prior to the meeting. Often school staff members will prepare a draft IEP prior to the meeting. You have a right to request a copy which will help you with your own planning.

- **Focus on the top priorities for your child.** Since an IEP will be developed for your child every year, there may be many skills that he or she needs as in the course of growing and maturing, but we encourage you to focus on the top priorities for your child as you decide on the goals. Identifying and prioritizing needs allows education to be adapted to the individual learner.

- **Plan your strategy for negotiation in advance.** Start by writing a list of the critical needs that must be covered in your child's IEP. Talk to his or her teacher and find out if you agree about the needs and priorities. If not, gather information to support your position. This could be work samples or expert reports from physicians, therapists or tutors. Think about the end result you want for your child. Don't get caught up in specific details of how the school will achieve the result. Let the school own the responsibility of coming up with the detailed plan of how it will help your child. You should be in agreement with the plan, but the school has to implement it.

Kelly's Story

Kelly has a severe communication disorder, autism and behavioral issues. Her mom wanted to request a one-on-one aide but was afraid the school would insist that Kelly be sent to the center school that was miles away. (A center school is designed to serve one population of students, such as children with disabilities or gifted students.) Both of Kelly's parents were opposed to having their daughter ride a bus for an hour, and it was financially impossible for her mom to drive 50 miles every day to get her there and back.

Kelly's mom sent her list of priorities to the school in advance of the IEP meeting. But as she continued to prepare, she decided she wanted our help. We asked her to gather as much information as she could prior to the meeting—where and when it would be held, and who would be there. She sent an email to the school requesting copies of any documents and any drafts of the IEP that would be used in the meeting. We reviewed the data from the school, and it seemed to support the request for additional personnel. We learned that the school had invited the ESE Executive Director who had the ability to give the budgetary authority to hire a paraprofessional. Then we made a list of what we thought the school might say or do, and how the family would respond. We also talked to as many people on the team as possible to try and figure out what was happening

81

behind the scenes. We knew the school wanted to make a significant change but no one would tell us exactly what it was going to propose. We went into the meeting prepared for the worst case scenario.

The outcome of the meeting was exciting. Rather than sending Kelly to a center school, the team's education members proposed moving Kelly to a classroom that would be more developmentally appropriate. They agreed to use an additional paraprofessional who would provide continuous adult supervision for Kelly at all times. Finally, they agreed to try an iPad as a new communication device in the classroom since Kelly was using one at home successfully.

Kelly made great gains that year and her parents were thrilled.

- **Know when to bring in experts.** Most parents are bright, knowledgeable people but sometimes their suggestions regarding what their child needs are ignored. As frustrating as this may be, bringing in a person regarded as an expert by the school team may be the answer to getting what the child needs to be successful in the classroom.

- **Understand that there may be a hidden agenda.** Do you know what we mean when we say a hidden agenda? A hidden agenda means people have an ulterior motive for their actions. What they are saying or why they are saying it masks what they truly think or feel. Although the IEP meeting should be focused on the child's needs, the development of the plan impacts everyone on the team. In some cases, individual team members may be thinking about how they will be personally affected by the changes in the IEP rather than how the child will benefit.

For example, regular education teachers and special education teachers may be thinking, "How on earth am I going to be able to do that when I have 25 other children?" We have heard such concerns voiced in actual meetings: "I know what he needs, I just don't have the time to do that in the classroom!"

A good, positive way to deal with this kind of situation is to ask team members direct questions in order to lead them to the outcome you desire– getting the appropriate services for your child. An example of a direct question: "Mrs. Jones, does Tommy struggle in reading in your class?" If she says yes, then ask: "What do you feel would help Tommy be successful? Do you have the resources you need to implement that for Tommy?"

The last part of the question is important. You want to make sure the team provides support for the front line educational staff. That way you can leave the meeting knowing the teachers will be able to deliver what was agreed upon because they will have the resources they need.

- **Know who the decision makers are.** Although IEP meetings are designed to reach outcomes collaboratively, often there is someone in the room who has the authority to be the ultimate decision-maker. This person can allocate school resources that may be necessary to help your child to succeed. It may be a representative from the district office, an assistant principal, or possibly even the principal. They have a hidden agenda: managing limited resources, staying on budget and considering an entire student population when making decisions. Knowing who they are will help you to aim your points toward them. If you can convince them—

get them on your side—the battle is usually more than half won.

Some people have dual roles in a meeting. You will be told their official title, such as teacher or therapist, but they may also have been assigned an "unofficial" role such as the gatekeeper. What does this mean? The gatekeeper helps to preserve the school's resources by making it very difficult to prove that a child needs a certain service, like a piece of equipment or a high frequency of therapy visits to make progress. If you feel an undercurrent in the room or see body language such as quick eye contact when certain things are discussed, those are indicators that there may be a hidden agenda in play.

Kyle's Story

Kyle was a brilliant student but he had executive function difficulties. He needed assistance with organizing information, managing materials, and understanding expectations. It was very helpful when teachers provided him with concrete examples and made sure that he had complete directions and accurate due dates for homework assignments.

Kyle had been going to the same school for a number of years and met with success as long as there was appropriate support in place. In the beginning of ninth grade, however, a new exceptional student education (ESE) teacher and a new paraprofessional were assigned to work with him. Unfortunately, the paraprofessional shared many of Kyle's organizational issues, making it difficult for her to support him. The new ESE teacher was overloaded with classroom responsibilities so her time to monitor Kyle's situation was limited. She was unable to oversee the work of the paraprofessional on a daily basis and the situation spiraled out of control very quickly.

Kyle's mom attempted to support his organizational needs from home. She contacted the teachers repeatedly, scheduled many meetings and became frustrated as her efforts were unsuccessful and Kyle's grades plummeted.

After many meetings that involved staff from multiple levels the team agreed to try and use technology to help with the organizational issues. By the time the school year came to a close, several solutions had been tried, but nothing had been resolved.

In tenth grade, there was yet another new ESE teacher and the same paraprofessional. Their attempts to implement the system designed in ninth grade failed to work. Kyle's mom felt strongly that the aide was more detrimental than helpful and had her stop going to his classes. The team started using email to communicate but it was not consistent. Finally, the assistant principal (AP) took over the job as liaison between home and school. However, she was retiring, so Kyle's mom knew there needed to be a different answer for the eleventh grade.

But when she requested a meeting with the new AP before the start of school so that everything would be in place for a successful eleventh grade, she was told by school personnel that AP would not be available until after the beginning of the year.

Kyle's mom decided not to take "no" for an answer. She emailed the assistant principal directly, who was quite receptive to meeting before school started. That was the first clue that there were internal communication issues at the school about this situation. She had also been told that the school was insisting that the same paraprofessional would be back in class with Kyle. This was the most critical issue that needed to be resolved because Kyle was not willing to go back to school if the aide was going to be there. She decided to take an advocate with her to the meeting.

The educational attendees consisted of the new AP, another new special education teacher, and the ESE liaison (she had been the special education teacher in 9th grade). The AP tried to take control of the meeting immediately by telling Kyle's mom that, if she would not agree to let the aide travel with Kyle every day, then the administration would not be willing to meet with her in the future to discuss this issue.

Even after years of dealing with this issue, Kyle's mom felt very emotional. She asked the AP if she wanted to review the box of data (an entire banker's storage box) that showed why having that aide in the room did not work. She also asked the ESE liaison to substantiate her reasons. The liaison was unable to give any data but assured the team that she had worked with the aide over the summer and that things would be better.

Then, the advocate spoke up and gave the AP the Reader's Digest version of what had transpired over the past two years. She explained that the school was proposing to replicate a service delivery model that didn't work before and had resulted in a horrific ninth and tenth grade year for Kyle. To top it off, the school wanted to have the same paraprofessional, who could not do the job the first time around, try it again.

Kyle's mom and the advocate could see the moment when the AP realized that she did not have all the facts from her staff. The ESE liaison had a hidden agenda. She thought that Kyle and his mother were the problem, not the services the school was providing, even though there was a box filled with evidence to the contrary. She also did not have any other ideas of how to solve the problem, and she did not want the paraprofessional to lose her job if the team decided her services were no longer needed.

That was a turning point. Kyle's team had established credibility, recapped the history succinctly and without getting emotional, and realized that a member of the staff was trying to pull the wool over the eyes of the new AP by blaming student and parent.

As a result, the new AP was able to get to the bottom line, put the child first and solve problems. She proposed a system to get the information home through the new ESE teacher without using the paraprofessional. It turned out that the new ESE teacher was also able to work with the other teachers and communicate effectively between school and home. The team set Kyle up for success. His junior year was his best year ever!

This story illustrates once again how important it is to keep good records. Kyle's mom had spent two years collecting data, following up regularly and keeping track of Kyle's progress. She went to the meeting with a clear strategy and knew what outcome she desired. She was willing to hold staff accountable and had facts to support her position.

She also knew when to call in an advocate and ask for help. That decision led to the revelation of a hidden agenda and someone present who knew what to do about it. When you are faced with a similar situation, look for the underlying issues and don't hesitate to contact an advocate or attorney if you feel these services are warranted.

- **Know the laws pertaining to your child's situation.** Many times the professionals attending a meeting think they are familiar with "policy," but they have never actually read the law. If you have, you will often be the most knowledgeable person in the room. Proving your point by using data or referencing written policies or laws can be the most effective means to get your way.

Emma's Story

Emma, a young girl with autism, was in a very challenging situation. Although her classroom teacher was energetic, she was on her first assignment since she graduated from college. A book smart teacher, she was still learning how to put into practice what she had been taught.

Emma's mom had been very patient throughout the year with the ups and downs. She understood that educating Emma was a complex process and worked hard with the school team to create a good environment where her daughter could make progress with her communication and learn how to learn.

At the beginning of the year, Emma's class had four children with a teacher and an aide, but by April the number of students had doubled. At the IEP meeting, Mom requested an extra paraprofessional be added to the classroom so that Emma could have more time with direct intervention from an adult. The data indicated that Emma required more one-on-one instruction time in order to make progress. It would also help the new teacher manage the growing number of students.

The principal reacted violently to the request. "We do not do that in this county!" she said. "We have a formula for aide support, and I am not going to add anyone else to that classroom."

Although shaken by the response, Emma's mom calmly explained why she was asking for the extra help and showed examples of Emma's lack of progress. The principal sat at the table shaking her head no. She insisted that if she granted extra help in this case, then every parent would want more personnel for their children.

The advocate spoke up and told the principal that the purpose of this IEP meeting was not to discuss the needs of her school as whole. Rather, the participants should stay focused on Emma's individual needs and how the team could work together to make sure she was getting a free appropriate public education.

The principal responded by asking the advocate, "What planet do you live on?" Then she yelled that budgets were very tight that year and she did not have extra money to add an aide to the classroom.

Although the advocate acknowledged the principal's concerns about finances and tried again to return to the purpose of the meeting, there was nothing she could say that would allow the conversation to move forward. At that point, the advocate requested the ESE Liaison make sure the parent's request was documented on the Prior Written Notice and spell out why the school was refusing the request. She further demanded that the Prior Written Notice reflect the reason the parent was turned down for additional aide support was due to budgeting restrictions. The ESE Liaison was familiar with compliance regulations and she knew what the principal said to the parent was not legal, but the principal was her boss.

After the meeting, Emma's mom was justifiably upset, not to mention furious. She went home and started calling private schools that specifically serve students with autism. She toured campuses and talked to other parents about their experiences there. With only two weeks left in the school year she decided to pull Emma out of the public school and enroll her in a private alternative the following year. Since Emma and her family lived in Florida, they had the option to apply for a McKay Scholarship that would pay most of the tuition at the private school and did not have to file a due process complaint to get the school district to pay for the placement.

The bottom line, Emma's mom, with the help of her advocate, knew her rights, behaved like a professional and asked for what her daughter needed. Even after doing everything right, she was not able to secure a successful outcome, however, and she had to decide whether to put her energy into fighting the school or looking for a different place for her daughter to attend. Fortunately, she found an alternative school setting that was more appropriate and enrolled Emma in the new school. The last we heard, Emma was making remarkable progress and the parent felt good about her decision.

Highlights

- Find out the purpose and agenda for all meetings with the school before agreeing to attend.
- Prepare for the IEP meeting by reviewing records, evaluations, reports and drafts of the IEP.
- Plan ahead, set your priorities and know what you want.
- Attend the meeting but bring someone with you. DO NOT GO ALONE!
- Set your emotions aside and stick to the facts.
- Be aware of hidden agendas in meetings.

- Have data to support your position.

- Prior Written Notice is a powerful tool to document a parent's request for services and the school's response to implement or deny the request.

Getting Ready

- Review your child's current IEP and progress reports from the past year to see if your child has mastered the goals. If some goals were not mastered, determine why so you can make changes for the next year.

- Review all other documentation that may be relevant to the upcoming meeting and use flags or a highlighter to make it easy to find information you may need to use in the meeting. (Remember: Never write on your original documents!)

- Make a list of your child's priority educational needs.

- Make a list of the talking points you want to discuss in the meeting with the team so you can check them off as you go through the meeting.

Magers and Spencer

Chapter 7

Understanding the IEP in Detail

A goal without a plan is just a wish.
—Antoine de Saint-Exupery, French writer

Now that we've presented an overview of the major issues in IEP meetings, we want to get more into the nitty gritty. If some of the information seems repetitive, it's because we want to approach it from another perspective.

Each IEP meeting has someone who is responsible for accurately completing the paperwork, placing it in the cumulative file, ensuring that everyone signs the IEP and making sure the team follows compliance procedures. The person's title may change from school to school. You must identify the person in your meeting filling this role.

Attending an IEP meeting can be intimidating and emotional. There are ways to make it a more pleasant and productive experience.

Bring food. It does not have to be anything fancy—just a plate of cookies, a fruit salad or a box of chocolates. Food helps everyone relax and generally leads to a friendlier atmosphere.

Be prepared. Make sure that you have taken time to review all the information you have about your child or that the school has provided to you prior to the meeting. Have your list of questions, concerns and suggestions in a written format so that you are ready to get down to business.

Say thank you. When you get your turn to speak in the meeting, start with the positives. If staff members have been working well with your child or going out of their way to help, be sure to acknowledge their work. Everyone appreciates being appreciated.

Let your child attend. Typically, everyone behaves better and remains focused on needs when the child in question is present. Your child does not have to stay for the whole meeting if that would not be appropriate, but being there for at least the introductions at the beginning of the meeting can be a very powerful statement. At a minimum, have a picture of your child on the front of your record keeping binder as a visual reminder of the true purpose of the meeting.

Notice

You already know that you should receive a written notice from the school before every IEP meeting, providing the date, time, location and purpose. It should also include a list of the people who have been invited to attend.

Review the notice carefully. Do the date and time work for you? If not, let the school know as soon as possible and provide them with options that will fit your schedule. The school must work with you to find a mutually agreeable time.

Do you know everyone on the list? If not, send an email to the person coordinating the meeting and ask about the unfamiliar people, what positions they hold, and the reason why they were invited.

Who will be attending the meeting with you? You are not required to tell the school in advance if you are bringing someone but we highly recommend you extend that courtesy to the team by indicating the name of the person and title on the Notice. The school does not appreciate surprises any more than parents do.

There are many different reasons a school may call together the IEP team besides the annual planning session. The purpose of the meeting could be:

- Parent Conference
- Eligibility Meeting
- Annual IEP
- Transition IEP
- Re-evaluation Review
- Discontinuation of Services
- Dismissal from Program
- Manifestation Hearing

Preparation

Since you have already been through the chapter on preparing for the meeting, you should have already reviewed all the records, evaluations, reports and the draft of the IEP. You have a list of what you feel are your child's priority needs and have thought about the strategy you will use when negotiating with the team. Remember to take along your record keeping binder in case you need data to help support your position.

Arrival

Try to get to the school about 15 minutes before the start of the meeting. This will give you time to park, find the location and collect your thoughts. You don't want to have to walk into a room full of people who are obviously sitting there waiting for you. IEP meetings are an important part of the school team's day, but it does interrupt instructional time and you will have a better working relationship with staff if you show that you value their time.

Introductions

The meeting should start with everyone being introduced. If there are a lot of people in the meeting, or people you have never met, it might be helpful to take notes as they say who they are and their purpose for attending. After introducing yourself, ask for business cards from people you don't know so that you have their contact information.

A well-organized facilitator will follow the introductions by telling the team the time allotted for the meeting, the agenda and the ground rules. If the person leading the meeting tries to move right to the IEP document, gently ask the timeframe for the meeting and in what order topics will be covered. Make sure the agenda allows for time to address your questions and concerns.

Parents are equal partners in the IEP process and should be treated that way. However, school personnel often think of having the parent at the meeting as a formality so the school can read them the draft IEP and get their signature. They have invited you so they are complying with the law but they don't really expect you to participate in the process.

Attendance

Everyone the school lists on the Notice to attend the meeting must be present for the meeting to take place, unless the parent excuses the person from the meeting. As the meeting progresses, participants may be excused if the team no longer requires their input as long as the parent and the school agree.

Signatures

At the first IEP meeting to place your child into the special education system, the school must have informed consent. The goals that are written and the placement indicated can only happen after you come to agreement and sign the document. After the initial IEP, your signature on future IEP documents only indicates that you were present for the meeting and does not mean that you consent with or agree to the final version.

So, go ahead and sign the document at the beginning of the meeting. But, according to *www.wrightslaw.com*, a website for reliable information about special education law and advocacy for children with disabilities, if you disagree with the contents of the IEP document, you should take a ballpoint pen and put the IEP on a hard table top and write this statement: "I consent to this IEP being implemented but I object to it for the reasons stated in the meeting." Then sign your name. This is the only time we will tell you to write on an original document.

Do not be surprised if someone on the school team gets upset and tries to tell you that you can't write on the document. You are a member of the team and you have the right to state your objections and they should be documented on the original IEP. Keep writing even if someone tells you to stop or tries to pull the document out of your hands. Make sure to get a final copy of the document before you leave the meeting. If they object strenuously, tell them that you have the legal right to do so, and they should look it up.

When you get home, write a thank you letter or email to the team members. Make sure you restate that, even though you have objections to the IEP program proposed, you have given permission for them to implement the plan. You want them to put some program into effect, even if the program continues to need to be refined or even replaced.

Parents' Concerns

At some point in the meeting, hopefully before you start writing goals for your child, the team will ask for the parents' concerns. You should have a concise list of priorities for your child that you can hand to the team. Having a well thought out typed list shows your professionalism and helps build your credibility as an equal member of the team.

You should have a second copy of the list for your own use, to make sure as you review and develop the goals for your child, that your concerns have been considered and addressed.

Present Levels of Performance

The present levels of performance section of the IEP contains a summary of your child's current academic achievement and functional abilities based on grades, evaluations and observations that give the team a benchmark as it begins to develop goals for the next year. The data should come from a variety of sources and show your child's performance in multiple environments including report card grades, scores on standardized assessments, evaluation information and staff observations.

Do you have data from outside experts that work with your child that should be incorporated into the present levels? If so, please try to provide copies of the information to the school a few days prior to the meeting. Having time to review the information outside of the meeting will allow the team to be more prepared to help your child.

In the Present Levels section of the IEP there should also be a statement about how your child's disability affects involvement and progress in the general education curriculum.

Special Factors

The team must consider any special factors that will impact your child's learning or the learning of others and indicate those factors in the IEP document.

The team must consider:

- The child's behavior and whether it impedes his or her own learning or that of others. The team must consider the strategies, including positive behavior intervention, and the support needed to address that behavior.
- The child's language needs. A child with limited English proficiency also may have special learning needs.
- The child's possible need for Braille. If a child is blind or visually impaired, the team must consider a provision for instruction in Braille.
- The child's communication needs. If a child is deaf or hard of hearing, the team must consider his or her communication and language needs.

- The child's requirements for assistive technology devices and services in order to meet educational goals and access the general education curriculum.

The special factors are usually addressed in a separate section of the IEP and should be considered when goals are written for your child.

Annual Goals

Annual goals, written specifically for your child, address what he or she needs to accomplish in order to make progress in the general education curriculum. Other goals regarding functional needs that result from your child's disability should also be considered.

You want goals that are written so all involved understand what they need to do, how it should be done, where it should happen, who will monitor progress and what your child should be able to accomplish at the end of the year. A stranger should be able to read the goal and know what your team intended.

Such goals ideally have five components. They should be:

S pecific
M easurable
A ttainable
R ealistic
T imely

The acronym SMART may help you to remember the five elements. Examples of SMART Goals would be:

Leslie will be able to read a grade-level passage and answer ten comprehension questions with 90% accuracy on four out of five opportunities.

John will use adapted equipment in physical education class with assistance of a personal care aide to participate in all activities with his grade level peers.

Communication

There should be an indication on the IEP of how often progress on the goals will be reported to you, the person responsible for the reporting, and how the progress will be measured. Teams often want every goal to be measured by teacher observation. Observation can be very subjective and may not be consistent from one teacher to the next. Whenever possible, encourage the team to use a concrete measurement tool that can be compared across environments such as a data collection sheet, weekly quiz or reading inventory.

Negotiating

In an IEP meeting you will negotiate a contract with the school to define the services that will be provided to your child to meet his or her specific needs. The school-based IEP team will probably start the meeting with a draft document to save time. Hopefully, you had a copy of the draft prior to the meeting and have reviewed the information and are prepared to discuss your concerns. Stick to your list of priority needs and insist on talking about each one of them.

Ideally, school staff and parents will work together in a collaborative manner, value each other's input, and come to agreement on what needs to be in the document. If your team struggles with collaboration, you've already learned how to prepare for the meeting so that you can present your case. Here are a few more ideas that will help you become a better negotiator:

1. Know what you want.

2. Stay focused and be consistent.

3. Be prepared with data and information to support your points.

4. Be flexible where you can but stay firm where it matters most.

5. If you have an expert with you, turn the floor over to that person to explain your request.

6. If you come to an impasse, table the issue and go on to the next. Come back to the area of disagreement after you have worked through all the other issues.

7. Use silence. State your requests concisely and then be quiet and wait for a response.

8. Consider where you are sitting in the room. If you know the person who is the ultimate decision-maker, sit next to them at the table.

9. Be conscious of your language. Try to use "we" so that you are seen as part of the team instead of referring to the school staff and your family separately. For example, "Thanks for the meeting today. I am confident we will be able to write a solid plan to meet John's needs."

10. Relay confidence by maintaining eye contact when you are speaking and listening. Be polite, courteous and professional but don't back down on the important issues.

Prior Written Notice

There are only two possible outcomes when you ask for something. The rest of the team agrees with you and adds it to the IEP or the team disagrees and they tell you no. If they say no, they must write what you requested on the Prior Written Notice document, tell why they refused, and what they will do instead to meet your child's need.

On occasion, you will run into someone in an IEP meeting that says, "We don't do that here!"

Remember that the team should be focusing on your child's unique needs and deciding how those needs can be served, rather than on making it easier or more economical for the teacher or the school.

Then, you might say, "I understand that you may not have done this before, but the team needs to consider my request. In order for my son to get his needs met, I think we need to try _____. Please tell me more about why you feel this would not work to help my son."

Finally, after further discussion, if the school refuses to do what you request, ask to have the discussion recorded on the Prior Written Notice.

Parents and schools need to work together in the best interest of the child; however, in the IEP negotiation process it may feel like the family vs. the school.

Talking about data and facts rather than showing emotions and placing blame when you are in disagreement about how to help your child will help you maintain the relationship with school staff.

Services

Once the team has written goals for your child, the next step in the meeting should be to determine the services needed for your child to make progress. There are several different categories of services that will be addressed.

Special Education—specially designed instruction to meet the unique needs of the child with a disability and provided at no cost to the parents. This can include instruction in the classroom, in the home, in hospitals and in other institutions.

Related Services—would include transportation and such developmental, corrective, and other supportive services as may be required to assist a child with a disability to benefit from special education.

Things that fall under related services include:

- speech-language pathology
- audiology services
- interpreting services
- psychological services
- physical and occupational therapy
- recreation
- social work services
- school nurse services specialized to meets the needs of the child with a disability
- counseling services including rehabilitation counseling
- orientation and mobility services
- medical services (for diagnostic and evaluation purposes only)

Supplementary Aids and Services—such as aids, services and other supports that are provided in regular education classes to enable your child with a disability to be educated with their non-disabled peers to the maximum extent appropriate in accordance with the law. A few examples are reducing distractions, use of a study carrel, textbooks for use at home, or providing peer buddies.

Transition Services focus on improving your child's academic and functional achievement to allow them to move from school to post-secondary education, employment, independent living and community participation. The process is results-oriented and considers your child's strengths, preferences and interests based on his or her individual needs.

Transition services include instruction, related services, community experiences, training in what is expected by employers and in other post-school adult living situations. When appropriate, it means working on daily living skills and a functional vocational evaluation. Transition services must be considered when your child turns 16, but can be worked on at a younger age, if appropriate. (HINT: It is always appropriate!)

Accommodations and Modifications

Accommodations are instructional or test adaptations that allow the student to show what they know without changing what is being taught in the classroom or measured on a test. An accommodation changes how or where information is presented but does not reduce the expectation of what the student will learn.

An example of accommodations would be reading test questions aloud to a student with a learning disability or allowing a student with attention issues to take a test in a separate room.

Accommodations are provided in the regular education classroom to level the playing field and allow the student with a disability to access the general education curriculum. Your child's accommodations should be listed on the IEP. Accommodations allowed in the classroom may be slightly different than what can be used on a standardized test. The example above about reading the questions aloud may not be an acceptable accommodation on a test that measures the child's reading ability.

Modifications reduce what a student is expected to know. A modification would include reducing the amount of work the student has to produce or simplifying the expectations for an assignment. Think very carefully before you agree to modifications. You want to hold your child and the school to high expectations. Always strive to put in place accommodations to allow your child to have the maximum access to the general education curriculum before you even consider allowing modifications.

Placement

Placement refers to where your child will receive instruction during the school day. Technically, the IEP team cannot talk about placement until goals are agreed upon and the team has decided on the necessary services. However, schools often start discussing placement before the IEP meeting because everyone wants to know "where" the child will go to school. If the team wants you to agree to a specific program or placement before the meeting they are denying you meaningful participation in the IEP process. This is not legal!

If this happens, thank the school for the information regarding the program or placement and decline to get into the discussion prior to working through the goals in the meeting. Maintain the relationship with staff but do not be bullied into making a decision outside of the IEP meeting and following the process prescribed by law.

There may be a variety of placement options to consider when determining where to best meet your child's educational needs.

The team must place your child in the least restrictive environment. What does that mean? To the maximum extent appropriate, your child must be educated with their non-disabled peers. A special class or separate school can only be considered when the nature and severity of your child's disability would prevent them from benefitting from their education with supplementary aids and services.

Every time you write a new IEP, various placement options should be considered. Just because your child has been in a special class or separate school for a period of time does not mean that your team should disregard considering a less restrictive environment. A really smart educator once said to us, "There is not a separate adult world."

Concluding the Meeting

At this point, you should have a completed IEP document. Your work is done! Well, not really. When you get home we advise that you send an email to the rest of the team members thanking them for their time and encouraging them to let you know if they have any concerns about implementing the IEP as written. Also, remind them you are always happy to hear about progress on the goals and will look forward to receiving a progress report in the time frame that has been agreed upon.

Follow-Up

Put a note in your calendar to remind you when to expect a progress report. If you do not get the information, send a request to school. Once you have it, make sure to review the data you have been collecting since the IEP to ensure it matches the report.

If not, call a team meeting to address the discrepancies. Address issues as they come up rather than allowing them to turn into a crisis.

Although IEP documents are written on an annual basis, the team can reconvene at any time if something needs to be changed or updated. Use your team's time efficiently and only request a meeting if absolutely necessary. If parents and the school staff are in agreement about a change, the document can be amended without a meeting.

Highlights

- Review the notice for the IEP Meeting carefully and respond to the school and let them know if you are available or need to reschedule.

- Tell the school in advance who will be attending the IEP meeting with you.

- Everyone listed on the notice must attend the IEP meeting unless the parent excuses the person from the meeting. If you do not want them excused, then the meeting must be rescheduled.

- Bring your record keeping binder to the meeting.

- Gather contact information for each person at the meeting so you can reach them afterwards if you have questions or concerns.

- Consider your child's future plans for post-secondary education, employment and independent living when developing their IEP.

- Be prepared to provide the team with a concise list of educational priorities for your child.

- Provide copies of data from outside experts to the school team a few days prior to an IEP meeting.

- Annual goals should be written to address what your child needs to make progress in the general education curriculum and to meet your child's functional needs that result from their disability.

- Learn negotiating skills.

- Prior Written Notice is a powerful tool.

- Accommodations level the playing field in a general education classroom.

- The IEP team cannot talk about placement until the goals have been written and the services have been determined.

- After the IEP meeting, write a thank you note to the team members.

Getting Ready

- Review the Resource List in the Appendix for more information on IEP meetings, writing SMART IEP goals and negotiating.

- Review the IEP Notice and respond to the school. If anyone unfamiliar is listed on the Notice to attend the meeting, ask the school to clarify who they are and why they have been invited.

- Find out more about Prior Written Notice.

- Put a note in your calendar to follow up on progress monitoring reports.

Magers and Spencer

Chapter 8

Resolving Conflict

Good intentions might sound nice,
but it's positive actions that matter.

—Tim Fargo
Author of *Alphabet Success*

Sometimes parents and schools do not agree. Each side feels like it is right and loses sight of staying focused on the best interest of the child. This leads to conflict instead of collaboration. Although the law makes provisions for schools and families to resolve their differences, we suggest that before you move toward a formal complaint resolution process, take a step back and examine your position.

Advocating for your child to get what is needed to be successful in school can raise your emotional state. You may want a specific curriculum, a piece of equipment or a service and the school disagrees. Sometimes you have been treated poorly by a staff member and you really just want an apology or an admission of wrong doing. You may feel that your child was misunderstood and perhaps mistreated—rather than seizing an opportunity for a positive teaching moment, the staff responded punitively. Whatever the case, take time to really think about why the problem occurred and what it will take to resolve the situation.

Whenever possible, try to remove the emotions from the debate. There are many reasons why a school and parent may disagree with legitimate concerns on both sides. For example, the school may not want to provide a service because of economic realities; the child may have severe behavior problems which require other resources than the school can provide; a parent knows a particular teacher or aide is not helpful and wants to be heard.

On the other hand, there are unreasonable people in any large organization. Some in positions of authority may like lording their power over parents and children and exercise their control just because they can get away with it. Sometimes a parent may have no idea why a problem has developed.

We know families that have been subjected to intimidation tactics by schools. These maneuvers can be quite subtle. Phone calls and emails from the mom are ignored. Parent/teacher conferences and other meetings are repeatedly cancelled. Staff shows a lack of sensitivity when delivering information. Parents are told they can't see their child's school records.

Worse things can occur. Schools and staff exercise zero tolerance. Students are suspended, expelled, or arrested. The school calls in Child Protective Services to investigate the home. Parents are banned from the school. Restraining orders are filed. We hope you never experience any of these tactics, but if you do, you need to be prepared.

Barbara's Story

Barbara advocated tirelessly for her son with attention deficit hyperactivity disorder (AD/HD). She was in constant communication with the staff and others at the district level seeking help. The school refused to cooperate with her and called Child Protective Services to investigate her. An agent came to her house, interviewed her child and found nothing out of line. Barbara was furious. She had done nothing but follow the rules in speaking up for her child. It was the school that upped the ante.

Barbara felt she had to respond in kind. She hired an attorney who was able to help her and the school reach an agreement, but she was not happy about incurring legal fees.

Barbara worked hard after the incident to rebuild the relationships with her son's teachers. She has never forgotten how she was treated by some of the staff and will always be cautious when dealing with this school, officially and unofficially. But it was in her son's best interest that she figure out how to work with the school staff after the problem was resolved.

You are protected by federal law from being punished for advocating for your child. However, proving retaliation can be difficult. Complaints can be made to the Office of Civil Rights but its staff members have specific criteria they adhere to when making a determination.

If an incident occurs, you need to document the circumstances and reach out to the appropriate school personnel to try and resolve the situation. You should also review the student handbook and code of conduct, look at your county's policies and procedures, research State Board Rules, and review federal statutes to locate the rules that apply to your situation.

The staff at your district office often has expertise that can help the school and parent resolve conflicts. Ask if anyone else should be called in to help because knowing "who" to talk to can get the problem fixed much more quickly. If you feel that the situation has escalated beyond your ability to solve the problem, consider calling an advocate or attorney.

Bring recurring problems that seem to be systemic to the attention of the school board. Also, media attention can make a difference when nothing else has worked and the problem affects more than one child. School systems are very sensitive to public airing of difficulties with parents. But use this option only as a last resort, because you will invite media scrutiny as well and must be prepared for it.

Sandy's Story

Sandy was attending a meeting out of town when she got a phone call from her daughter's school, asking her to come get her daughter immediately because she was destroying the classroom and had kicked the teacher. This was highly unusual behavior and had never happened before.

Sandy drove for two hours to pick up her daughter and scheduled a meeting at the school for the next day to talk about what had happened and to do a functional behavior assessment. Sandy had built relationships with staff at the district level so she asked the school to invite a district staff member to help facilitate the meeting.

When Sandy arrived at the meeting she was greeted at the door by the principal of the school and the school resource officer. Sandy was told that if her daughter behaved like that again they would call the police to arrest her. In the state of Florida kicking a teacher constitutes a felony.

Sandy was stunned. She thought she had a good relationship with the teacher. She had been giving the teacher daily tips on what worked best to help her daughter learn and she even considered the teacher a friend.

The meeting came to an abrupt end. Sandy never found out what had caused her daughter's outburst, and there hasn't been one since. Sandy left the meeting and went to the school district offices to meet with the exceptional student education director. He made a phone call to another principal and Sandy's daughter moved to a new school.

When a meeting deteriorates, you have two options. You can take a break and excuse yourself to regroup or stop the meeting and reschedule. Don't get discouraged; there will always be ups and downs. And remember to consider the best outcome for your child in any given situation.

When all goes wrong

There are times, however, even when you follow all the rules and heed our recommendations, that you may not be able to move the mountain. At that point you will need to engage in a more formal complaint resolution process.

Learn your due process rights and responsibilities by reading the Procedural Safeguards that are given out at IEP meetings. Schools have the responsibility to have someone explain them to you if you don't understand them. The document clearly outlines the remedies for resolving problems. The most common avenues for filing a complaint are due process or a state complaint.

If the school team refuses to initiate or change the identification, evaluation or education placement of your child with a disability, or does not provide your child with a free appropriate public education (FAPE), you can file a due process complaint and request a hearing before an impartial hearing officer. This is a legal process and we highly recommend you retain a lawyer to represent you. Due process must be filed within two years of the violation of the special education law and can only be initiated by the parent or the school district.

At the hearing, the parents and the school district staff each present their version of the facts. Each side may present documents, oral testimony and subpoena witnesses to support their cause. The rules of evidence are in effect and you must follow formal court procedures throughout the process. Once the hearing has taken place, the hearing officer must issue a decision within 45 days. If you disagree with the hearing officer's findings you may appeal to state or federal court.

Within 15 days of requesting a due process hearing the school district must invite you to a meeting to discuss the complaint and try to resolve the dispute. There is also a mediation process that you may try prior to going to the hearing in lieu of having the meeting.

A trained mediator with no affiliation to the school district will facilitate the mediation session. Parents and the school district staff will each be given an opportunity to present their position and supporting documentation to the other party. The mediator will attempt to help the two sides come to a mutually agreeable solution. If you can find common ground, the mediator will write up a binding agreement that will be followed by both parties. If you cannot come to agreement, then you proceed to the hearing.

Going through a due process hearing can be very difficult both emotionally and financially. Legal costs can run into the tens of thousands of dollars and the outcome may not be favorable. Statistically, school districts prevail much more often than parents. We are not saying that you should never consider due process but you must educate yourself about the costs and the likelihood of a successful outcome before you begin this effort. Sometimes, you have no choice but to take this action for your child but you need to be prepared for the long haul and know exactly what you are trying to accomplish in the end.

A state complaint can be filed by any individual or organization that feels a school has violated any state or federal education law. Such a complaint must be filed within one year of the occurence and will be investigated by the state Exceptional Student Education staff to determine if there was a violation of law. The ESE staff must make a determination within 60 days. If a violation is found, the school district will be ordered to take corrective action. Be aware that a state complaint cannot be appealed. However, the investigator may consider new or additional information that has bearing on the investigation.

A state complaint can be filed regarding an issue concerning your own child or a more general issue that affects many other children. There are numerous resources available online that can help you put together a state complaint.

If you have reached the point that you need to take formal action, find an attorney, advocate or another parent who has been through this process to help you decide whether to file a due process complaint, state complaint or both. Gather information and reach out for assistance before you make the next move.

Highlights

- Take the steps necessary to advocate for your child including the use of formal complaint procedures but remember at the end of the day, when the problem is resolved, it is in your child's best interest if you make the effort to rebuild relationships with school staff.

- Don't threaten to file a complaint unless you are prepared to proceed.

Getting Ready

- Research and make a list of attorneys, advocates and other parents in your area who have expertise in working successfully with the school system.

- Go to *www.idea.ed.gov* and explore the website to become familiar with the federal law governing services for children receiving special education.

- Obtain a copy of your Procedual Safeguards from your school if you don't have one already.

Chapter 9

Continuing On

*The man who moves a mountain begins
by carrying away small stones.*
—Confucius, *Chinese philosopher*

Throughout this book we have shared many suggestions regarding developing skills and employing strategies that we have personally found helpful for ourselves and the many parents with whom we have worked. Once you have mastered these skills and strategies, they will serve you in whatever situation you may encounter. Start by thinking about the skills you already have and how you can apply them to solve your current problems.

There are two resources we use often when we need additional information about special education law and processes. The first, www.wrightslaw.com, is published by Pete Wright, a special education attorney from Virginia. The information is presented in parent-friendly language and will help you understand the application of laws and regulations related to the IEP process. The second site, www.idea.ed.gov is maintained by the US Department of Education and provides the public with the latest changes in federal law related to special education.

We hope that you feel inspired to become a committed advocate for your child. Trust yourself and your instincts. By building a strong support network, making your relationships a priority and educating yourself by reading books and learning from others, you will become equipped to champion your child's cause. When necessary, ask for help and involve expert consultants.

You may be surprised that you will evolve a new mindset. Embrace it! By remaining calm, persevering, picking your battles and taking authority with a grain of salt, you will become a professional advocate in your own right. And you will find it easier to take personal responsibility by planning ahead, being prepared and informed. Remember, information and knowledge gives you power.

Never forget that parents are the only people with a long-term interest in their children. Many teachers and administrators who work in the school system want to help, but their concern and interests may not be the same as yours. Don't believe everything you are told; trust but verify. Keep in mind that developing an IEP is a negotiation and that everything is negotiable.

Having a person centered plan for your child will help guide your decision making. Ensuring your child has a functional means of communication should be your top priority. Focus on what your child can do, and concentrate on your child's strengths and interests. This will point you in the right direction.

Learn to value the process. Appreciate the small victories and find joy in the life you are living with your child. Give yourself permission to take a day off and have fun. Take care of yourself so you can continue to be your child's champion.

The conclusion of this book is not the end, but the continuation of your journey to help your child succeed.

Get ready and go move mountains!

Appendix A

Getting Organized

Following up from Chapter 3, here is what we recommend you purchase and prepare to be optimally organized:

1. Two-inch, three ring binder
2. Three hole punch
3. Self-stick divider tabs
4. Sheet protectors

   - Put all of your child's school records for the year in the binder in reverse chronological order.

   - Use divider tabs to indicate the first page of important documents like the IEP or assessment information so you can get to them easily in a meeting.

   - Use sheet protectors to save samples of your child's work that you want to share with the team as evidence to demonstrate your position.

5. Set up a log to keep track of conversations with teachers and other staff. It can be just a piece of notebook paper in your binder with the following headings:

Date	Time	Who I spoke with?	What was said?

Under "What was said?" make sure to note if an action is going to be taken. List what will be done, who will do it, and how/when the results will be reported.

If you have a conversation with someone and you want to create a paper trail, send that person a follow-up email to thank them and clarify what you understood was going to happen afterwards.

For example:

Dear Mrs. Smith,

It was a pleasure to speak with you this afternoon and I appreciate you sharing your concerns about Johnny's reading grades. Based on our conversation, I understand you will now be sending Johnny to the reading specialist two times per week during the reading block for more individualized instruction to see if it helps him to improve his grades. In addition, you would like me to read with him for at least 30 minutes, four times per week.

I look forward to working with you to help Johnny. I will also follow up with an email each Friday to check on Johnny's progress and will meet with you again in four weeks to see if the plan is working.

Thank you,

Sarah Jones

Appendix B

Glossary

504 Plan. The "504" in "504 plans" refers to Section 504 of the Rehabilitation Act of 1973 which specifies that no one with a disability can be excluded from participating in federally funded programs or activities, including elementary, secondary or postsecondary schooling. "Disability" in this context refers to a "physical or mental impairment which substantially limits one or more major life activities." This can include physical impairments, illnesses or injuries, communicable diseases, chronic conditions like asthma, allergies and diabetes, and learning problems. A 504 plan spells out the modifications and accommodations that will be needed for students to have an opportunity to perform at the same level as their peers, and might include such things as wheelchair ramps, blood sugar monitoring, an extra set of textbooks, a peanut-free lunch environment, home instruction, a tape recorder or a computer tablet for taking notes.

Accommodations are changes that can be made in the way a student accesses information or demonstrates performance. These changes can be made to the learning environment or how educational materials look, but do not affect standards or levels of curriculum.

Advocate is a person who speaks or writes in support of, on behalf of, or in defense of another person or cause.

ASD Autism spectrum disorder (ASD) refers to a group of developmental disabilities that can cause significant social, communication and behavioral challenges.

Assistive Technology is any item, piece of equipment or product system that increases, maintains or improves the functional capabilities of a child with a disability.

Bureaucracy is a body of non-elected government officials and/or an administrative policy-making group. Bureaucracy refers to the administrative system governing any large institution. It is characterized by diffusion of authority among numerous offices and all-too-often inflexible adherence to rules of operation.

Center School is a school designed to serve one population of students, such as children with disabilities or gifted students.

Chain of Command is the order of authority or power in an organization. In a school district you should communicate first with the person in charge of the class or program. Then move on up to the school based administrator, the district administrator and then the school board. The best way to communicate is by email or phone. Emails and phone numbers can be found on school and district websites.

Charter School is an alternative education system in which a school receives public funding but operates independently.

Compliance means that schools must follow education rules, policies and procedures established at local, state and federal levels. Additionally, schools, districts, and county offices that receive funding for certain programs may be chosen for a review by the state. The purpose of the review is to ensure that they are spending the funding as required by law. Reviews may take place in person and/or through an online process. At the end of each review, the state will complete a report of findings and informs the school, district, or county office how to correct the findings.

Conflict Resolution employs certain techniques, collaborators, and mediators use to resolve disagreements between parents and educators, especially in the area of special education. The goal is for the resulting settlement to provide maximum benefit to children with special needs.

Consent requires that the school district get written permission before evaluating a student. The district must also get written consent before providing special education services for the first time. Parents must be informed in a language they can comprehend, and they must agree in writing to the action and understand that it is voluntary. Consent can be revoked or withdrawn at any time.

Determination according to the dictionary is the act of making or arriving at a decision. In special education this could refer to determining that a child is eligible to receive special education services. It could also be a decision reached by a hearing officer in a Due Process hearing.

Disability is defined in the Individuals with Disabilities Education Improvement Act (IDEIA) and includes 13 primary terms under the main definition of "a child with a disability." These federal definitions guide how states define who is eligible for a free appropriate public education under special education law.

Draft IEP (Individualized Education Program) is a proposed IEP. It does not prevent parental input and should be provided to the parent well in advance of the IEP meeting.

Due Process refers to the parental right to resolve disputes with a school district and is defined in the Individuals with Disabilities Education Improvement Act (IDEIA).

Due Process Hearing is a legal procedure to resolve disputes between parents and schools involving an administrative hearing before an impartial hearing officer or administrative law judge.

Educational Records under the Federal Rights to Privacy Act (FERPA) are defined as records that are directly related to a student and are maintained by an education agency or institution or by a party acting for the agency or institution. The information may be recorded in any way, including, but not limited to, handwriting, print, computer media, videotape, audiotape, film, microfilm, microfiche, and e-mail.

Elder Care Attorney is not a technical or legal title. Elder Law and Special Needs Law are defined by the clients to be served. In other words, the attorney who practices Elder Law or Special Needs Law works primarily with people as they age and people with disabilities.

Evaluations are procedures used to determine whether a child has a disability and the nature and extent of the special education and related services that the child needs.

Exceptional Student Education (ESE) is educational programs and services for students with special learning needs. This is sometimes referred to as special education.

Exceptional Student Education (ESE) Liaisons are usually staff members in the school system whose job it is to assure IEP teams are in compliance with local, state and federal guidelines and may serve as the LEA representative on the team.

Executive Function is a set of mental processes that helps us connect past experience with present action. This includes activities such as planning, organizing, strategizing, paying attention to and remembering details and managing time and space.

FAPE (Free Appropriate Public Education) is special education and related services provided in conformity with an IEP. It is offered without charge and meets standards of the State Education Agency (SEA).

Federal Regulations (CFR) is the codification of the general and permanent rules and regulations (sometimes called administrative law) published in the Federal Register by executive departments and agencies of the federal government of the United States.

FERPA (Family Educational Rights and Privacy Act) is a federal statute about confidentiality and access to education records.

Financial Planners are professionals who engage in what is commonly known as personal financial planning. In carrying out the planning function, they are guided by the financial planning process to create a financial plan—a detailed strategy tailored to a client's specific situation, for meeting a client's specific goals. Financial planners consider all questions, information, and advice in light of its impact on the entire financial and life situation of the client.

Functional Behavioral Assessment (FBA) is a process for collecting information that will help determine the underlying purpose or motivation of a student's behavior that proves challenging or interferes with learning (examples: seeking attention, peer acceptance, avoiding, etc.).

Functional Needs children may have physical, sensory, mental health, and cognitive and/or intellectual disabilities affecting their ability to function independently without assistance.

Functional Performance generally refers to activities and skills that are not academic or related to a child's academic achievement as measured on achievements tests.

Gatekeeper is a person who controls access to something. The term refers to individuals who decide whether a given message will be delivered to people with decision making power.

General Education is a curriculum adopted by a Local Education Agency (LEA) or State Education Agency (SEA) for all children from preschool through high school.

Goals are objectives that spell out results or achievements toward which effort is directed. In Special Education, goals are developed to be able to measure an individual student's progress.

Guardian is one who is legally responsible for the care and management of the person or property of a minor or someone adjudicated as incompetent.

Guidance Counselor is an educator who works in elementary, middle, and high schools to provide advice regarding academic, career, college readiness, and personal/social competencies to all K-12 students through a school based counseling program.

IDEA or **IDEIA** are both acronyms referring to the Individuals with Disabilities Education Improvement Act of 2004, which assures all students with disabilities access to the general education curriculum. The act recognizes that special education is a service and not a place, and provides for a broad range of services addressing the needs of all students with disabilities. It provides a continuum of options for a student with a disability alongside non-disabled peers and assures that parents are informed participants in education decision making with due process rights.

IEP stands for **Individualized Education Program** (also called an Individualized Education Plan). This is a legally binding document that spells out exactly what special education services your child will receive and why. The IEP is developed at an IEP meeting.

IEP Meetings are required by federal statute. They are convened at least once a school year to plan an educational program that is tailored to the needs of each child with a disability. The child's "team" attends the meeting: teachers, therapists, parents, school administrators, and any other invited parties.

Independent Education Evaluation (IEE) A parent has the right to an independent education evaluation at public expense if the parent disagrees with an evaluation obtained by the public agency. However, the public agency may initiate a hearing to show that its evaluation is appropriate. If the final decision is that the evaluation is appropriate, the parent still has the right to an independent education evaluation but not at a public expense.

Informed Consent A school cannot perform an initial evaluation, place a child in a special education program, or reevaluate a child without receiving the parent's permission in writing. Consent is voluntary and may be revoked at any time.

Intervention is additional instruction and teaching strategies that enable struggling students to improve their academic performance in the area that they are having learning difficulties.

Job Coach is a person, usually supplied by an outside agency, who provides specialized on-site training to employees with disabilities. Typically, a job coach will help employees learn to perform their jobs accurately, efficiently and safely. In many cases, the job coach may also help the them acclimate to their work environment.

LEA is an acronym for **Local Education Agency** or school district.

LEA Representative is the person who represents the school district at an IEP meeting and has the authority to allocate district resources needed to implement the IEP.

Learning Disability is a neurological condition that interferes with a person's ability to store, process, or produce information. Learning disabilities can affect one's ability to read, write, speak, spell, compute math, reason and also affect a person's attention, memory, coordination, social skills and emotional maturity.

Least Restrictive Environment (LRE). To the maximum extent appropriate, children with disabilities are educated with children who are not disabled. Removal of children with disabilities from the general education environment occurs only when the nature or severity of the disability is such that education in general classes with support cannot be achieved satisfactorily.

McKay Scholarship in Florida is a school choice program for children with disabilities designed to allow parents to choose the best public or private educational setting. The McKay Scholarship Program also offers parents public school choice. A parent of an eligible special needs student may choose to transfer the student to another public school.

Measurable Annual Goals are statements that describe reasonable expectations of what a child can accomplish from the specialized educational program during the school year. They set the general direction for instruction and assist in determining specific courses, experiences, and skills a student will need to reach his or her goal. There must be a direct relationship between the goal and the needs of the student, and it must be possible to evaluate the results in a quantifiable way.

Mediation is a procedural safeguard to resolve disputes between parents and schools. It must be voluntary, cannot be used to deny or delay the right to a due process hearing, and must be conducted by a qualified and impartial mediator who is trained in effective mediation techniques.

Modifications are substantial changes in what the student is expected to demonstrate in instructional level, content and performance criteria. They may include changes in test form or format and include alternate assessments.

Multidisciplinary Centers are based at a participating university and offer clinical services, including diagnosis, assessment, and intervention planning for children with disabilities and their families. They also provide early intervention services, pre-service training, and outreach training, and they conduct research. All developmental disabilities are addressed, with an emphasis on children birth to five years of age. Available professionals include: developmental pediatricians, psychologists, and social workers, with access to occupational therapists, physical therapists, speech-language pathologists, and special educators.

Notice is a way of telling parents about an action the school plans to take that will affect their child's education. This may be by letter, phone call, email, or other means.

Occupational Therapy often called OT, is the use of treatments to develop, recover, or maintain the daily living and work skills of people with a physical, mental or developmental condition. Occupational therapy interventions focus on adapting the environment, modifying the task, teaching the skill, and educating the client/family in order to increase participation in and performance of daily activities, particularly those that are meaningful to the client.

One-on-one aide/support occurs when schools assign dedicated aides to support the education of students in various situations. Supplementary aids and services are required "to enable children with disabilities to be educated with nondisabled children to the maximum extent appropriate…" Some of the most common reasons for this support include protection/safety of the student, instructional support, transition, and reduction of anxiety for the student.

Outside Agency Providers and their representatives may be invited to the IEP transition-planning table. There are four primary agencies in adult services: Vocational Rehabilitation, the Social Security Administration, state-level agencies, and independent living centers. There is an "other" category as well—other players and groups you may want to involve.

Paraprofessional is an umbrella term for various educators, also known as para-pros, paraeducators, instructional assistants, educational assistants, teacher's aides or classroom assistants. These teaching related positions within a school exist to generally provide specialized or concentrated assistance for students in elementary and secondary schools. Not all states have a fixed definition of "paraprofessional" and may use all of the terms listed above, and many others, interchangeably.

Personal Care Assistant (PCA), commonly known as caregiver, personal care attendant, patient care assistant, personal support worker and home care aide, refers to paid employees who help persons who are disabled or chronically ill with their Activities of Daily Living (ADLs), within or outside the home. They assist clients with personal, physical mobility and therapeutic care needs, usually as per care plans established by a rehabilitation health practitioner, social worker or other health care professional.

Physical Therapist or **physiotherapist** (sometimes abbreviated to PT or physio) is a health care professional primarily concerned with the remediation of impairments and disabilities and the promotion of mobility, functional ability, quality of life and movement potential through examination, evaluation, diagnosis and physical intervention.

Placement refers the type of setting where a student will receive special education services. These services may be provided in various locations through the day based on the individual needs of the student.

Positive Behavioral Support (PBS) is a decision making framework that guides selection, integration, and implementation of the best evidence-based practices for improving important academic and behavior outcomes for all students.

Postsecondary refers to the stage of learning that occurs at universities, academies, colleges, seminaries and institutes of technology.

Present Level of Educational Performance (PLEP) is a summary describing the student's current achievement in the areas of need as determined by an evaluation. The PLEP contains specific, measurable, objective baseline information for each area of need affected by the disability. In addition, it links the evaluation results, the expectations of the general curriculum and the goals for the student.

Prior Written Notice is the required written announcement to parents when the school proposes to initiate or change, or refuses to initiate or change the identification, evaluation, or educational placement of a student.

Priority Educational Need is a statement written on the IEP that specifies the most important needs for your child. IEP goals should be linked to the priority educational needs.

Private School is a school that does not get any money from the government and is run by a private group and usually charges tuition and fees.

Procedural Safeguards are requirements outlined in IDEIA, giving parents the right to participate, receive notice and give consent. Parents also have the rights to ask for an independent educational evaluation, examine records, and request mediation and due process.

Progress Monitoring is the ongoing collecting and analyzing data to determine student progress. Progress monitoring should be used to make instructional and service decisions based on student performance.

Reevaluations occur at least every three years from the time of a student's initial evaluation/initial eligibility for Special Education. The purpose is to determine if the student still has a disability and if the services being provided are appropriate.

Regular Education or **General Education** is the program of education that most students participate in and includes academic and vocational classes. General Education is now the default placement, since the passage of the reauthorization of IDEA in 2004, now called IDEIA. The act mandates that all children should spend a significant amount of time in a general education classroom, unless it is not in the best interest of the child, or because the child is a danger to him/herself or others.

Related Services are services that are necessary for a child to benefit from special education. They include speech-language pathology, audiology services, psychological services, physical and occupational therapy, recreation, early identification and assessment, counseling, rehabilitation counseling, orientation and mobility services, school health services, school nurse services, social work services, parent counseling and training.

Reverse Chronological Order is putting items in date order from what happened most recently and working back to the earliest dates.

School Improvement Plan is the development and implementation of strategies and steps used by a school to raise student achievement.

Self–Advocacy concerns the actions people with disabilities take to be sure their needs are understood and met, their wishes are respected and their rights are honored. It also refers to the civil rights movement for people with developmental disabilities (also called cognitive or intellectual disabilities) and other disabilities. Self-advocacy is also an important term in the disability rights movement, referring to people with disabilities taking control of their own lives, including being in charge of their own care in the medical system. The self-advocacy movement is (in basic terms) about people with disabilities speaking up for themselves.

It means that although persons with a disability may call upon the support of others, they are entitled to be in control of their own resources and how they are directed. It is about having the right to make life decisions without undue influence or control by others.

Self-Determination a characteristic of a person that leads them to make choices and decisions based on their own preferences and interests, to monitor and regulate their own actions and to be goal-oriented and self-directing.

Sib shops are workshops or seminars designed for siblings of persons with special needs. They reflect a belief that brothers and sisters have much to offer one another, if they are given a chance. Sib shops are a spirited mix of new games (designed to be unique, off-beat, and appealing to a wide ability range), opportunities to make new friends, and discussion activities.

Social Worker is a professional dedicated to improving the social, emotional and academic outcomes for all students.

Special Education is a term that covers all specially designed instruction, at no cost to parents, to meet the unique needs of a child with a disability. It includes instruction conducted in the classroom, in the home, in hospitals and institutions, and in other settings; and instruction in physical education.

Specially Designed Instruction (SDI) refers to ways that special education professionals adapt the content, methodology (approaches to teaching certain grade level content), or the delivery of instruction to address the unique needs that result from a child's disability. Specially designed instruction should ensure that the child has access to the general curriculum so that he or she can meet the educational standards that apply to all children.

Speech-Language Pathologists (SLPs) are professionals who specialize in communication disorders as well as in swallowing disorders.

Standardized Testing refers to any test given in the same manner to all test takers. Standardized tests need not be high-stakes tests, time-limited tests, or multiple-choice tests.

Standard High School Diploma is awarded for the completion of high school. In the United States and Canada, it is considered the minimum education required for government jobs and the pursuit of higher education, such as entering university. An equivalent is the General Education Diploma (GED).

State Board Rules are statutes and rules pertaining to exceptional student education services adopted by each state legislature.

State Education Agency (SEA) is another name for the State Department of Education.

State Complaints are a mechanism through which individuals and organizations can address special education conflicts and resolve disputes. Each state is required to adopt written procedures for resolving any complaint that meets the definition of a State Complaint under Part B regulations of IDEIA.

Supplementary Aids and Services are support activities and programs that are provided in regular education classes and enable children with disabilities to be educated with nondisabled children to the maximum extent appropriate.

Support Groups are gatherings where participants provide each other with various types of help based on a particular shared, usually burdensome, characteristic. Members with the same issues can come together to share coping strategies, feel more empowered, and find a sense of community. The help may take the form of providing and evaluating relevant information, relating personal experiences, listening to and accepting others' experiences, providing sympathetic understanding and establishing social networks. A support group may also work to inform the public or engage in advocacy.

Support Network is a group of people available to provide assistance and usually consists of family, friends, community member, and paid professionals. If you were in crisis or needed help, who would you call? This is your support network.

Therapist is a person skilled in a particular type of treatment, designed to help and improve a person's physical and/or psychological wellbeing.

Transfer of Rights At the age of 18, educational rights transfer to eligible students. All procedural safeguards and rights held by the parents are guaranteed to the student.

Transition is a coordinated set of activities for a student with a disability, which promotes movement from school to post-school activities, including post-secondary education, vocational training, integrated employment (including supported employment), continuing and adult education, adult services, independent living, or community participation. It is an outcome-oriented process, based upon individual students' needs, taking into account their preferences and interests. Transition includes instruction, related services, community experiences, the development of employment and other post-school adult living objectives, and, when appropriate, acquisition of daily living skills and functional vocational evaluation.

Transition specialist is a school district employee with significant knowledge and information about the process of preparing a child to move from school to adult living. The specialist can help the school team find resources to support the child's individualized plan for independent living, employment and post-secondary education.

Transition Individualized Education Program is required when a student is about to enter high school or turns 14. Beginning at age 16 (or younger if appropriate) a statement of transition services needed by the student must be included in the IEP. This includes post-school goals for the world of work, post-secondary education and independent living.

U.S. Department of Education also referred to as ED (which stands for the Education Department) is a cabinet-level department of the United States Government.

Appendix C

Resource Guide

Books

Bateman, Barbara D. and Herr, Cynthia M., *Writing Measurable IEP Goals and Objectives.*

Farrall, Melissa Lee and Wright, Pamela Darr, *Wrightslaw: All About Tests and Assessments: Answers to Frequently Asked Questions.*

Siegel, Lawrence M., *The Complete IEP Guide: How to Advocate for Your Special Ed Child*, 8th Edition.

Spence, Gary, *How to Argue & Win Every Time: At Home, At Work, In Court, Everywhere, Everyday.*

Wright, Peter and O'Connor, Sandra, *Wrightslaw: All About IEPs: Answers to Frequently Asked Questions About IEPs.*

Wright, Peter, and Wright, Pamela, *Wrightslaw: From Emotions to Advocacy—The Special Education Survival Guide.*

Wright, Peter, and Wright, Pamela Darr, *Wrightslaw: Special Education Law*, 2nd Edition.

Ury, William, *Getting Past No: Negotiating in Difficult Situations*

Websites

www.copaa.org—Council of Parent Attorneys and Advocates

www.idea.ed.gov—Building the Legacy: IDEA 2004

www.ndrn.org—National Disability Rights Network

www.pacercenter.org—Pacer Center—Champions for Children with Disabilities

www.wrightslaw.com—Special Education Law website

Acknowledgments

Our families—thank you for your support over all of these years. We appreciate your tolerance when we spent our days going to meetings and evenings on the phone with other families. Your love and encouragement to be agents for change helped us to keep going.

Lee Byron—for your efforts in starting the first Parent Liaison program and recognizing that parents need someone in their corner.

Our fellow parent liaisons: Jan DeBoer, David Ursel, Gerald Robinson, Laura Hughes, Chris Resch, Holly Anthony, and Teresa Johnson—each of you made a difference. We couldn't have made it through this journey without you.

School district partners—thank you for believing in the services we provided and that having someone support families made a difference in the outcomes for the students.

The many families whose lives we touched—thank you for putting your trust in us to be part of the team and allowing us to help you create positive outcomes for your child.

Community partners – especially Family Network on Disabilities (FND Manasota) for the many collaborative opportunities to provide parent education programs.

Sue Memminger—thank you for your love, ideas, and support. You can be on our island anytime.

Susan and Mac McFarland—you generously allowed us to hunker down in your condo and write without intrusion from the outside world. We are forever grateful for your kindness.

Our early readers—thank you for offering your input, feedback and encouragement to keep going. Your suggestions helped shape *Moms Move Mountains*.

All the parents and professionals who offered testimonials— thank you for your confidence in the information in this book and its value for families.

Chris Angermann—thank you for helping us publish the book. Your belief that we had a manuscript worth sharing encouraged us to take it out of the trashcan and make it available to other families. We so appreciate your guidance and insightful editing skills. You showed us how to shape our rough draft into a product we are proud to share. It would not have been possible without your talent and dedication.

For further information

go to

www.MomsMoveMountainstheBook.com

www.ingramcontent.com/pod-product-compliance
Lightning Source LLC
Chambersburg PA
CBHW022025090426
42739CB00006BA/296